BEYOND GLASS CASES:

THE LIBRARY COMPANY OF PHILADELPHIA'S "COLLECTIONS LAB"

BEYOND GLASS CASES: THE LIBRARY

COMPANY OF PHILADELPHIA'S

"COLLECTIONS LAB"

BY DANIEL TUCKER

With contributions from Bill Adair, Linda Kimiko August, Rachel D'Agostino, Mark Thomas Gibson, Emily Guthrie, Sharon Hildebrand, Tania Isaac Hyman, Zachariah Julian, Shannon Mattern, Paul Wolff Mitchell, Erika Piola, Tafari Robertson, John C. Van Horne, and Sarah Weatherwax.

COMMON GROUND

First published in 2025
as part of the **Arts in Society Book Imprint**

Common Ground Research Networks
University of Illinois Research Park
2001 South First St, Suite 201 L
Champaign, IL 61820 USA

Library of Congress Cataloging-in-Publication Data
Names: Tucker, Daniel, 1983- author
Title: Beyond glass cases : the Library Company of Philadelphia's
   "collections lab" / by Daniel Tucker.
Description: Champaign, IL : Common Ground Research Networks, 2025. |
   Includes bibliographical references. | Summary: "Beyond Glass Cases   represents the Library Company's ongoing commitment to boldly, honestly,   and thoughtfully interpret challenging, and at times harmful, collection   items. An independent research library founded in 1731 and specializing   in American society and culture from the 17th through the early 20th   centuries, the Library Company has collected books and graphics   throughout its almost 300-year history. Today, the Library is faced with   the task of finding new and better ways of advancing understanding and   engaging public awareness of the complex histories of these challenging   collection items, while still holding space for their historical   significance"-- Provided by publisher.
Identifiers: LCCN 2025039277 | ISBN 9781966214922 hardback | ISBN
   9781966214939 paperback | ISBN 9781966214946 pdf
Subjects: LCSH: Library Company of Philadelphia | Collection development
   (Libraries)--United States--Evaluation | Library exhibits--United States
   | Libraries--Public relations--United States
Classification: LCC Z733.P551 T83 2025
LC record available at https://lccn.loc.gov/2025039277

ISBN: 978-1-966214-92-2 (HBK)
ISBN: 978-1-966214-93-9 (PBK)
ISBN: 978-1-966214-94-6 (PDF)

DOI: 10.18848/978-1-966214-94-6/CGP

Cover Image Credit: barb barnett graphic design llc

Credit List for BGC Publication Photographs

@Jaci Downs Photography: p. 2, p. 3 top/bottom, p. 4 bottom, p. 5 top/bottom, p. 6 top/bottom, p. 40, p. 41 top/bottom, p. 42 top/bottom, p. 43 top/bottom, p. 44 top/bottom, p. 45 top/bottom, p. 46, p. 63 top/bottom, p. 65 top/middle/bottom, p. 66 top/middle/bottom, p. 89, p. 92 top, p. 93 top/bottom, p. 94 top/bottom, p. 95 top/bottom, p. 112, p. 113 top/bottom, p. 114 top/bottom, p. 115 top/bottom, p. 116 top/bottom.

Sharon Hildebrand: p. 4 top, p. 64 top/bottom, p. 90 top/bottom, p. 91 top/bottom, p. 92 bottom.

Max Macdonald Photography: p. 67 top/bottom,
p. 68 top/bottom.

TABLE OF CONTENTS

FOREWORD

John C. Van Horne
Director, Library Company of Philadelphia

The Library Company's 2022 grant application for "Beyond Glass Cases: The Library Company of Philadelphia's 'Collection Lab'" described the project as "an initiative designed to drive adaptation of the Library Company's exhibitions program and its capacity to engage a broad and diverse audience in the exploration and ever-evolving interpretation of its collections."

We are grateful to The Pew Center for Arts & Heritage for funding "Beyond Glass Cases," which represents the Library Company's ongoing commitment to boldly, honestly, and thoughtfully interpret difficult, and at times harmful, collection items. And we have plenty of those! Since our founding in 1731—fast approaching 300 years ago—the Library Company has acquired hundreds of thousands of books, pamphlets, broadsides, manuscripts, graphic works, and art and artifacts. Given the vast changes over that long spell in the sensibilities and sensitivities of different ages, it was inevitable that among those acquisitions there would be some that to our twenty-first-century eyes are distasteful, perhaps even offensive. Yet as a repository and responsible steward of historical materials, the Library Company could never contemplate discarding such materials or hiding them from the scholars of various disciplines who choose to engage with them.

Rather, through "Beyond Glass Cases," we are bringing them into the light to be studied as artifacts of previous centuries and reinterpreted by contemporary artists and historians. Through an invitation to the public, the Library Company chose creative partners who would transcend traditional exhibition models and find new and better ways of advancing understanding and engaging public awareness of the complex histories of these collection items while holding space for their historical significance.

"Beyond Glass Cases" showcased the work of four such partners—speculative historian Tafari Robertson; musician Zachariah Julian with anthropologist and historian Paul Wolff Mitchell; and visual artist Mark Thomas Gibson—as they created art works, curated exhibitions, and composed music in dialogue with Library Company material.

Tafari Robertson's project, "The Black Historians' Department: The Past Belongs to You," created a space dedicated to the Black historians who cultivate their practice and stories outside of traditional institutions. It was a speculation of what would be different about history as a form if it were built around the ways that Black people hold and exchange information with each other and what it means to amplify and support those processes. Robertson explored these ideas with other members of Philadelphia's Black artistic and cultural community in a series of workshops/listening sessions. The exhibition that grew out of these sessions included an office setting and a living room interior setting where visitors were invited to engage with reference books, audio tapes, and video clips as ways to experience history. Two cases of items from the Library Company's African American History Collection were also displayed. "The Past Belongs to You" was an invitation to understand Black history as a community practice, not to be discovered or authorized, but participated in.

The second element was "Project Obtuse," centered around the work of Samuel George Morton (1799–1851), whose papers reside, in part, at the Library Company. Morton is known today as among the most influential architects of scientific racism in the United States, both for his publications—most notably *Crania Americana* (1839)—and for his collection of nearly one thousand human skulls from across the world, amassed and measured during his lifetime to supply the "data" for these works. For "Project Obtuse," Jicarilla Apache artist Zachariah Julian used color, sound, and movement to confront this dark chapter in the history of indigenous peoples in America. He collaborated with anthropologist and former Library Company Fellow Paul Wolff Mitchell, who conducted a thorough study of the Morton Papers across several repositories and curated the exhibition "Crania Americana and the Archive of Scientific Racism". Together they explored how Morton's thinking developed and how his theories still affect us today. Through composition and performance, Julian shifted our gaze away from the past chapter written by Morton and his colleagues and toward a thriving present and future that Indigenous Americans write for themselves.

The third element was "Lineage," a series of four large-scale paintings by artist Mark Thomas Gibson, who examined the proposition of "the future of humanity" by responding to Samuel Jennings' 1792 painting "Liberty Displaying the Arts and Sciences (or The Genius of America Encouraging the Emancipation of the Blacks)." This large-scale painting, created by the artist as a gift to the Library Company, depicts the allegorical figure of Liberty offering various forms of knowledge to several recently enslaved Black figures in a posture of supplication before her. It has traditionally been described as the first painting by an American artist of an abolitionist theme and has had pride of place among the Library Company's collection of works of art. It has been lent for exhibition over the years and has appeared on the dust jackets or otherwise illustrated in books too numerous to count. In short, "Liberty" can quite accurately be described as "iconic." But more recently the painting has touched a nerve because of its depiction of the newly freed Blacks as grateful supplicants to a white figure in an even whiter dress who has broken their chains, seen lying at her feet. In the background are more Black figures in an "attitude expressive of Ease & Joy." Such was the late-eighteenth-century understanding of slavery and how its demise was envisioned. Artist Gibson held listening sessions with Philadelphia high school history teachers, high school students from the social justice media program POPPYN, community leaders attending the political education program Du Bois Movement School for Abolition & Reconstruction, and volunteers from the Paul Robeson House and Museum before creating his four remarkable paintings that reinterpret Jennings' work.

Following those three exhibitions, the "Reflections" exhibition took a look back at this many-faceted project to more fully explore our partners' creative processes in telling their stories about Library Company holdings and practices. "Reflections" also directly solicited reactions from our visitors about the broader questions raised by "Beyond Glass Cases," including the most fundamental one: What role should libraries and museums take in addressing social justice issues?"

We were pleased that Daniel Tucker accepted the charge of producing this summary publication that incorporates both an account of the several projects and the voices of those who shared their reactions with us. He is a producer of documentaries, publications, classes, exhibitions, and events at the intersection of art and politics, and his collaborative art projects have been published and presented widely.

Finally, a word about organizational structure. Virtually all the principals involved in conceiving the project and writing the grant application are no longer with the Library Company. Over the past two years or so, there has been an almost complete turnover of staff involved in the project, from the Director on down. The staff members who inherited the project are responsible for its success, and they should be given all credit for carrying out a project designed by others and ensuring that its original goals were met. Chief among them is Sarah Weatherwax, Senior Curator of Graphic Arts, who took over the project upon the departure of Librarian Emily Guthrie early in 2024. Ms. Weatherwax graciously accepted the direction of the project in addition to her regular duties.

She was ably abetted by staff liaisons Linda Kimiko August, Rachel D'Agostino, Wynn Eakins, Sharon Hildebrand, and Erika Piola.

"Beyond Glass Cases" has been a project unlike anything the Library Company had done previously. It was an opportunity to reexamine not only our collections but also our own attitudes toward the collections, and to gain an understanding of how members of those communities reflected in and affected by how particular collection items respond to them emotionally and artistically. For that we are grateful.

SECTION 1

In Context

Images: Events and Process Documentation from Beyond Glass Cases

How Artists Make History: "Beyond Glass Cases" in the Context of the War on Public Memory

By Daniel Tucker

Introduction

There is a bit of a difference between 3 years and 294 years. But regardless, what you hold in your hands is the result of a multiyear process. On one hand, it could be seen as the result of a library founded in 1731 spending 294 years thinking about its purpose. On the other hand, it is the result of a project developed out of a grant application that was awarded in 2022 and unfolded across three years.

The 294 timeline starts out with a Colonial-era institution established when it was increasingly common to form mutual-aid societies that would try to satisfy collective needs. In this case, the group was a discussion group called the Junto and the need was a library of useful books to share with one another, utilizing a first-of-its-kind (in the new colonies) subscription scheme for sharing books among "shareholders" of the library.[1] That organization, the Library Company of Philadelphia, came to be one of the most intact collections of eighteenth-century daily life, and so it remains today a valuable institution where the use value has shifted from books to help users in daily life to books that help users understand early American culture. This gradual shift from being a library to a research library has led to a deepening investment in presentation of archival holdings through exhibits and public programs.

One of the implications of this status shift is that the materials held within the collection necessitated greater interpretation to be understood in their historical context. This was a particular challenge for material that came to be understood as controversial due to the evolution of views over time. That evolution of views transpired in dialogue with social movements demanding a more transformative

---

[1] Liz Covart, "Episode 001: James N. Green, Librarian at the Library Company of Philadelphia," *Ben Franklin's World*, October 7, 2014, https://benfranklinsworld.com/001/.

politics of redistribution, but gradually through defeats and compromises settled for a politics of representation—though philosopher Nancy Fraser argues that both forms of justice are necessary and one shouldn't replace the other.[2]

So, for instance, a painting or a book may have been gifted by a shareholder in the early days of the institution reflecting commonly held prejudicial or derogatory attitudes in its depictions about races and sexes other than the white male constituency primarily served by the institution. Over time as society was forced to incorporate critiques of that racism or sexism into its public policy and cultural practice, the appeal and utility of these objects required a critical distance to understand. There were phases of brushing such complexity under the rug, and then more recently a confrontation with those holdings has begun to take shape led by those inside the institution as well as activists and artists from the outside who want to challenge historical institutions to rethink those histories and the implications of preserving them. That the collection at the Library Company spans such a long history and can be used to trace these compromised politics of redistribution and representation makes this project hold such great potential.

This gets us to the three-year timeline. The Library Company's administration sought out a grant from The Pew Center for Arts & Heritage to develop a series of interventions into objects within the collection that were controversial. This series of exhibits and events, titled "Beyond Glass Cases: The Library Company of Philadelphia's "Collections Lab," invited artists and scholars into the Library Company for creative residencies. Once there, they interfaced with staff liaisons and created projects using the collection as a prompt for their own work and deeper commitments.

The primary concern of this essay is to consider how libraries, archives, and museums can ethically and imaginatively present controversial objects in their collection and what role artists might play in that recuperation by reframing institutional narratives through experimental exhibitions and programs. Looking forward, the rest of the essay will offer contextualization for "Beyond Glass Cases" with consideration of the crisis of representation in libraries, archives, and museums, as well as the ethical tensions and political context that a project of this kind must face. This will set up the following two sections of the book to be a deep dive into "Beyond Glass Cases" where all the projects and participants will be given detailed attention.

[2] Nancy Fraser, Hanne Marlene Dahl, Pauline Stoltz, and Rasmus Willig, "Recognition, Redistribution and Representation in Capitalist Global Society: An Interview with Nancy Fraser," *Acta Sociologica* 47, no. 4 (2004): 376, http://www.jstor.org/stable/4195051.

The Crisis in Representation in Collecting Institutions

The "museumizing imagination" is what the historian Benedict Anderson has called the impulse to collect, represent, and narrativize the cultures of the world.[3] This impulse motivated many buildings to be built and artifacts to be acquired (traded, stolen, donated, and purchased) to house the material wealth of societies in their home and frequently abroad. As museum scholar Tony Bennett has discussed, in the shift from classical to modern organizational logics he reflected that

> the birth of the museum is coincident with, and supplied a primary institutional condition for, the emergence of a new set of knowledges—geology, biology, archaeology, anthropology, history and art history—each of which, in its museological deployment, arranged objects as parts of evolutionary sequences (the history of the earth, of life, of man, and of civilization) which, in their interrelations, formed a totalizing order of things and peoples that was historicized through and through.[4]

These emergent disciplines and their approaches to structuring knowledge have become the inherited logics of today's institutions.

Combined with the idiosyncrasies, fetishes, and biases of the founding figures of each library, archive, and museum—the DNA for each institution can be variously opaque or transparent for the contemporary visitor. As you walk through the door today you are more likely to be confronted with a rebranded image designed for easy legibility and public consumption rather than a contextualizing statement about where everything came from, how it was acquired, and what ideologies influenced its founders. Some institutions have explicitly set up their "difficult heritage," which the anthropologist Sharon Macdonald describes as "rather than emphasising times of the nation's glorious achievement...what was being flagged up were times of evil wrong-doing that did no evident credit to a positive national identity."[5] But for the most part this has not been the case.

---

[3] Benedict Anderson, *Imagined Communities: Reflections on the Origin and Spread of Nationalism* (Verso Editions, 1983, 1996 edition), 178.

[4] Tony Bennett, *The Birth of the Museum: History, Theory, Politics*, 1st ed. (Routledge, 1995), 96, https://doi.org/10.4324/9781315002668.

[5] Sharon Macdonald, "Is 'Difficult Heritage' Still 'Difficult'?" *Museum* 67 (2015): 6, https://www.tandfonline.com/doi/abs/10.1111/muse.12078

In the context of the United States, collecting institutions have long been associated with the elite, despite many internal initiatives to rethink their work and their collections. Beyond their founders, much of this has been stymied because of their fundamental orientation of board members and staff on the basis of their lived experience. As curator Kelli Morgan has written, "Representation works for White people within art institutions in ways that it does not for BIPOC because White representation and White middle-class cultural mores are inherent to every aspect of the functionality of dominant society. BIPOC representation and cultural values are not."[6] This critical observation has led to movements oriented toward both reform of existing institutions and a push toward the creation of new ones.

One early example of this reform variety is the 1968 initiative Art & Soul that developed in the deeply disinvested west Chicago neighborhood of Lawndale with the support of the newly created Museum of Contemporary Art Chicago. Art Historian Rebecca Zorach described the space as one that "served as a neighborhood art studio with classes for children, a library of books, freely available materials for artists, an artist residency, contests, readings, and exhibitions."[7] But what made it more than a museum doing education and engagement was that it was also a collaboration with the Conservative Vice Lords, a former street gang that had reorganized itself as a community-oriented service project only a few years prior while still retaining many aspects of its original culture. As Zorach explains, "It was a pragmatic bargain among organizations with rather different interests."[8] And it was hardly a revolutionary project as it made use of various grants that in many ways inhibited as much as facilitated the project. But it was an early example that offers a lot of lessons about partnership that are relevant to this day.

Describing the reform-oriented practices thirty years ago, Tony Bennett has described these objectives as "the demand that there should be parity of representation for all groups and cultures within the collecting, exhibition and conservation activities of museums, and the demand that the members of all social groups should have equal practical as well as theoretical rights of access to museums."[9] Later in his text Bennett suggests these goals toward "representational adequacy" are not achievable within the current institutions and that

---

[6.] Kelli Morgan, "How Can Museums Truly Shake off Their Colonial Legacy?" *Hyperallergic*, March 10, 2023, https://hyperallergic.com/806866/how-can-museums-truly-shake-off-their-colonial-legacy/.

[7.] Rebecca Zorach, "Art & Soul: An Experimental Friendship Between the Street and a Museum," *Art Journal Open*, September 4, 2011, https://artjournal.collegeart.org/?p=2104.

[8.] Zorach, Ibid.

[9.] Bennett, *The Birth of the Museum*, 9.

political effort would be better devoted to transforming the relations between
museum exhibits, their organizers and the museum visitor ... In addition to what
gets shown in museums, attention needs also to be paid to the processes of show-
ing, who takes part in those processes and their consequences for the relations
they establish between the museum and the visitor.[10]

This proposal foreshadowed the move toward community engagement efforts that have become increasingly prevalent in the field (and build on legacies of projects like Art & Soul). In 2015 the report "Museums, Libraries and Comprehensive Initiatives," attributes of this new community engagement direction were identified and ranged from deeper time commitment to embeddedness within community networks that allowed for approaches that exceeded the episodic and limited partnerships of previous eras.[11] This work has evolved to include community advisory boards, satellite locations, sliding scale admissions fees, and co-curation practices with community groups and local experts.[12]

Concurrent with this push toward community engagement are the impact of demonstrations for racial justice in 2014 following the brutal murder of Michael Brown by police in Ferguson (Missouri) leading to a national movement and within this sphere, prompting the social media campaign #museumsrespondtoferguson.[13] This push was intensified and widened in 2020 catalyzed by more brutal murders, this time of George Floyd and Breonna Taylor by local police in Minneapolis (Minnesota) and Louisville (Kentucky), respectively. The demonstrations and actions that followed foregrounded substantial conflicts over representation that continue to linger. In the library field, this manifested strongly in a call for conceptualizing and enacting practices of belonging. In her 2020 column for *American Libraries Magazine*, the librarian Meredith Farkas captured that aspiration as "When people see their identities represented and celebrated by their library, they are more likely to see the library as a space for them."[14]

---

[10] Ibid.

[11] "Museums, Libraries and Comprehensive Initiatives: A First Look at Emerging Experience" (IMLS/LISC, 2015), https://www.imls.gov/sites/default/files/publications/documents/museumslibrariesandcomprehensiveinitiatives.pdf.

[12] Daniel Tucker, "Engagement Curating" part 1 and 2, *The International Journal of the Arts in Society* 16, nos. 1, 2 (2024), https://cgscholar.com/bookstore/works/the-international-journal-of-the-arts-in-society-volume-16-issue-1; https://cgscholar.com/bookstore/works/the-international-journal-of-the-arts-in-society-volume-16-issue-2.

[13] Gretchen Jennings, Aletheia Wittman, Rose Paquet, et al., "Joint Statement from Museum Bloggers and Colleagues on Ferguson and Related Events," *The Uncatalogued Museum*, December 11, 2014, https://incluseum.com/2014/12/22/joint-statement-from-museum-bloggers-colleagues-on-ferguson-related-events/.

[14] Meredith Farkas, "Representation Beyond Books," *American Libraries Magazine*, March 2, 2020, https://americanlibrariesmagazine.org/2020/03/02/representation-beyond-books/.

At this same time of foment the Diversity, Equity, and Inclusion consulting field was well positioned to step in to support institutions who were rethinking their work and aspiring toward belonging. Like universities and corporations, collecting institutions also attempted to right historical wrongs through trainings, workshops, and organizational restructuring. And like any large push for cultural change, the effects of this were uneven.

One demand that had a long history but intensified at that moment of reckoning in 2020 was the aspiration toward repatriating objects taken from indigenous communities and conceptualizing decolonization within collecting institutions. As the museum educator Therese Quinn wrote at the time, "Decolonization begins by recognizing Native communities and the original inhabitants of the land, and extends to sharing the power to make decisions about exhibits, programs, and more, with justice as a central aim."[15] In the context of the United States, this allowed for many pushes to return and rethink human remains that were originally taken in the name of scientific racism[16] and as a matter of public policy to in 2023 finalize many aspects of The Native American Graves Protection and Repatriation Act that had yet to be realized since it was established in 1990.[17]

The activist, curator, and scholar La Tanya S. Autry co-initiated the global campaign #MuseumsAreNotNeutral to try to confront what she saw as the fundamental contradiction of the field.[18] Continuing with that insight, the museum advocate Vedet Coleman-Robinson wrote that

> interpreting culturally diverse stories and artifacts is not what divides us. What divides us is the omission of those stories under the pretense of neutrality. Teaching American history without the full truth is what creates division. Museums do not create division by presenting facts; they build understanding. They create space for dialogue, healing, and recognition.[19]

---

[15] Therese Quinn, *About Museums, Culture, and Justice to Explore in Your Classroom* (Teachers College Press, 2020), 30.

[16] Samuel J. Redman, *Bone Rooms: From Scientific Racism to Human Prehistory in Museums* (Harvard University Press, 2016).

[17] Office of Communications, "Interior Department Announces Final Rule for Implementation of the Native American Graves Protection and Repatriation Act," U.S. National Park Service, n.d., https://www.nps.gov/orgs/1207/interior-department-announces-final-rule-for-implementation-of-the-native-american-graves-protection-and-repatriation-act.htm.

[18] La Tanya Autry and Mike Murawski, "Museums Are Not Neutral: We Are Stronger Together," *Panorama*, Fall 2019, https://journalpanorama.org/article/public-scholarship/museums-are-not-neutral/.

[19] Vedet Coleman-Robinson, "First They Came for Black History," *Hyperallergic*, August 20, 2025, https://hyperallergic.com/1035834/first-they-came-for-black-history/.

The museum leader Laura Raicovich built on that work writing that

> *Neutrality [is the] persistent ideology within the museum. However, there are*
> *many structures…that are directly oppositional to any desire for diversity and*
> *inclusion…. The problem lies in the fact that these structures are unseen and*
> *unregistered…. If we truly want to undo barriers to inclusion, we must face this*
> *false neutrality and dismantle it.[20]*

After reviewing this history and participating in much of it, I cannot help but think that one of the deeper challenges of initiatives in recent years is imprecise language. Having mentored many students and young professionals with activist impulses, I can attest that there is nothing more frustrating than wanting a revolution within an institution that really only aspires toward diversifying attendance at their public programs. This takes me back to the enduringly useful breakdown of categories related to "Cultural Equity" by the blog Create Equity. In their 2016 collaborative writing they proposed that there are four archetypes of "Diversity, Prosperity, Redistribution, and Self-Determination" that account for the range of visions for equity in cultural organizations. They go on to explain them like this:

> *Diversity: Mainstream institutions become more diverse and reflective of their*
> *communities. Prosperity: Large-budget organizations focused on artists of*
> *Color present work to a broad audience. Redistribution: Funders provide more*
> *resources to organizations rooted in communities of Color. Self-Determination:*
> *People of Color have ownership over shaping cultural life in their communities.[21]*

The usefulness of this simple breakdown is that most likely a push toward Self-Determination at an organization that celebrates Prosperity will lead to a temporary rhetorical change that leads later to retrenchment. These kinds of tensions animated many campaigns for labor rights within museums that emerged following both racial justice organizing and the pandemic. It was, of course, challenging for workers to see their employers publicly claiming solidarity with mass social movements that they understood would not be tolerated internally

---

[20] Laura Raicovich, *Culture Strike: Art and Museums in an Age of Protest* (Verso Books, 2021), 12.

[21] Clara Inés Schuhmacher, Katie Ingersoll, Fari Nzinga, and Ian David Moss, "Making Sense of Cultural Equity," *Createquity*, 2016, https://createquity.com/2016/08/making-sense-of-cultural-equity/.

or professing a commitment to themes of care through their programming while simultaneously underpaying or undervaluing their staff.[22]

Fast forward to the present moment and the remnants and seeds of all of these past efforts remain, but there is a widespread and very public backlash. This has started with the confrontation of Critical Race Theory in school curriculum[23] and resentment of the 1619 Project's goal to reframe U.S. history "by placing the consequences of slavery and the contributions of black Americans at the very center of our national narrative."[24]

As of this writing in August of 2025, the administration of Donald Trump's second Presidential term has taken aim at the cultural heritage sector in a variety of ways. Starting in March of 2025, there was an Executive Order entitled "Restoring Truth and Sanity to American History," which specified the goal to

> *ensure that all public monuments, memorials, statues, markers, or similar properties within the Department of the Interior's jurisdiction do not contain descriptions, depictions, or other content that inappropriately disparage Americans past or living (including persons living in colonial times), and instead focus on the greatness of the achievements and progress of the American people or, with respect to natural features, the beauty, abundance, and grandeur of the American landscape.*

The text went on to suggest that the "Smithsonian Institution has, in recent years, come under the influence of a divisive, race-centered ideology."[25] There have also been extensive cuts to the National Endowment for the Arts (NEA), National Endowment for the Humanities (NEH), and the Institute for Museum and Library Services (IMLS)—the three pillars of cultural policy in the United States and the main sources of public funding that is redistributed to state and local arts and humanities councils.

The ripple effects have been immediate and national in scope. In Philadelphia these actions have resulted in several aspects of Independence National Historical

---

[22] Museums Moving Forward has compiled the Art Museum Unions Index which looks at organizing since 2019 in art museums specifically (though it is important to note that the trend has also taken place at other kinds of museums and libraries), https://museumsmovingforward.com/research/projects/union-organizing.

[23] For a thoughtful narrativization of this process listen to Emanuele Berry on This American Life episode 758. This American Life, "Talking While Black," May 16, 2025, https://www.thisamericanlife.org/758/talking-while-black.

[24] New York Times, "The 1619 Project," July 9, 2025, https://www.nytimes.com/interactive/2019/08/14/magazine/1619-america-slavery.html.

[25] The White House, "Restoring Truth and Sanity to American History," March 28, 2025, https://www.whitehouse.gov/presidential-actions/2025/03/restoring-truth-and-sanity-to-american-history/.

Park exhibits being flagged for review and potential removal. Specifically, some of the content that was deemed inappropriate was the exhibit "The Freedom and Slavery in the Making of a New Nation," which focused on George Washington owning enslaved people at his residence when the city was the first capital of the United States.[26] In Los Angeles many organizations working on documenting life in a rapidly gentrifying city lost their funding. One organization, the Los Angeles Poverty Department, which runs the Skid Row History Museum & Archive, lost IMLS, NEH, and California Humanities grants totaling almost 22% of the organization's annual budget.[27]

Back in Philadelphia, the Avenging the Ancestors Coalition, the group that originally rallied to create the exhibit about Washington and slavery, has been mounting a response. Their work advocating for this narrative had begun back in 2002, and it took until 2010 for the exhibit to be completed—a testament to the fact that these kinds of projects take years of painstaking work by advocates and scholars to be realized and are potentially being undone in a matter of months.[28] Some of the timing is intended to alter exhibitions and historic sites in advance of the 250th anniversary of the founding of the country, happening in 2026 nationally but with a significant presence in early colonial and revolutionary war locales like Philadelphia.

When discussing a 2020 project at the Brooklyn Public Library that sought to invite proposals for new amendments to the U.S. Constitution, called the 28th Amendment Project, Laura Raicovich proposed that these are exactly the kinds of projects that the sector needs to engage in, writing that "rather than a space of abstracted expertise, the cultural sphere should be understood by the public as a zone in which to negotiate issues we may not necessarily agree on."[29]

At this particular moment of crisis and culture war, the field needs bold and ambitious projects that take on the disagreements. In the coming years and throughout 2026 specifically, there will be numerous tests about the politics of telling truthful and complete histories.

---

[26] Evgenia Anastasakos, "The Trump Administration Is Considering Removing Independence National Historical Park Exhibits for Depicting American History in a Negative Light," Inquirer.com July 23, 2025, https://www.inquirer.com/politics/nation/independence-national-historical-park-exhibits-removal-trump-administration-20250723.html.

[27] Renée Reizman, "Casualties in Trump's War on the Arts: The Small Museums Keeping Local History Alive," *The Guardian*, June 3, 2025, https://www.theguardian.com/us-news/2025/may/25/small-museums-trump-cuts-arts-funding.

[28] Michaela Althouse, "Rally on Saturday Aims to Save Independence National Park Exhibit Threatened by Trump," *PhillyVoice*, August 2, 2025, https://www.phillyvoice.com/philadelphia-presidents-house-slavery-exhibit-rally-trump-administration/.

[29] Laura Raicovich, *Culture Strike: Art and Museums in an Age of Protest* (Verso Books, 2021), 38.

I am hopeful that there are some possibilities for greater collective action at this time—as there is more that cultural organizations have in common than the particularities of their missions might suggest. In recent months The National Coalition Against Censorship (NCAC) and the Vera List Center for Art and Politics (VLC) convened leaders from across the country to author a statement "Cultural Freedom Demands Collective Courage." The statement tries to respond to this moment when many organizations are facing pressure to change their programming and many are preemptively changing their work in anticipation of pressure. The statement proposes that "programmatic autonomy" in the face of this pressure and perceived pressure is essential to the work of supporting democracy as they facilitate "freedom of expression, encourage critical thinking, and create important opportunities for public discussion and dissent." One of the commitments the signatories of this statement make is to "stand with fellow institutions facing political pressure and remain a field united by shared values and principles."[30]

Another advocacy group, the BLIS Collective, wrote following President Trump's May executive order that

> What's needed now is not just outrage, but deeper investment in the civil and narrative infrastructure required to defend truth. We must mobilize resources for strategic litigation, coordinated advocacy, cultural production, and long-term power building. Museums and libraries need legal protection and visible public support, educators need policy safeguards, and cultural institutions need funders willing to act boldly, not freeze in fear.[31]

As the documentation of the "Beyond Glass Cases" project shows—there can be a significant amount of growth and discomfort in the process of truth telling. For an organization like the Library Company of Philadelphia, the tension of being simultaneously old and up for trying new things is admirable to tackle. But looking forward, many organizations of a similar profile are going to be cautious about interrogating their institutional, local, and national history with a critical lens. To offer some inspiration for those who might want to take up

---

[30] The National Coalition Against Censorship (NCAC) and the Vera List Center for Art and Politics (VLC). "The Statement - Cultural Freedom Demands Collective Courage: A Nation-Wide Statement of Values and Principles for the Field of Arts and Culture," 2025, https://www.collective-courage.com/.

[31] BLIS Collective, "Authoritarianism Starts with Erasing History: President Trump's Executive Order Targets Public Memory. We Must Respond," Press Release, May 19, 2025, https://www.bliscollective.org/blis-in-the-headlines.

the mantle of the Library Company and work with artists to intervene in their collections—the following section will introduce a number of precedents and tactics from the recent past that might inform future work.

Artists as Archival Interveners: Five Key Words, Ten Key Works, and Three Key Questions

Because there is such a wealth of examples, below I am going to briefly introduce a wide range of artistic strategies that have been used to critically engage the representation of history. Some examples will include artists who made their own collections of subcultural history while others involve artists who intervene in existing collections and artifacts, both invited and without permission. Some interventions are responding to authoritarian rule while others are playful as a method of generous invitation to see the world anew. This diversity of tactics should be useful to those seeking models of archival intervention to adapt to their own contexts.

To start, let us consider a few keywords, beginning with the word *archive* as both a verb and a noun. Looking at archiving as a site and as an activity will help in the consideration of how artists have engaged with archives in their work.

The next keyword grows from one fundamental concern many artists have, which is the power of the *frame*. Maybe it is something inherited from painting? But as it relates to archives, the power of the frame can be seen as the power of what is kept or not, and the awkwardness or curiosity of what is kept or not. It is about the parameters of the collection, from whom and where it is sourced.

And beyond keeping stuff, there are the questions of *use* (and utility). As the Interference Archive project in Brooklyn reminds us, "Use Is Preservation" because it keeps it alive.[32] And according to Sue Breakell, an archivist at the Tate in London, an archive is more than a collection: "the use of the term 'archive' is an assertion of the changed status of this material, which has gone from obscurity to preservation and presentation."[33]

And the frame is also in the power to assert *memory*, another keyword. It could be to intervene in an existing narrative of an institutionalized history, to propose

---

[32] Jen Hoyer and Josh MacPhee, "Interference Archive: Building a Counter-Institution in the United States" (Pound the Pavement #29/Interference Document 25, Self-published Risograph), January 2023, https://interferencearchive.org/what-we-do/publications/interference-archive-building-a-counter-institution-in-the-united-states/.

[33] Sue Breakell, "Perspectives: Negotiating the Archive," *Tate*, 2008, https://www.tate.org.uk/research/tate-papers/09/perspectives-negotiating-the-archive.

a micro-narrative that combats the grand narrative. This is one reason why curator Nato Thompson suggests artists have turned to archives and reenactment.
Thompson reflects that "Just as these artists query what we should remember,
they also pose the question how do we remember and how do we forget. Projects
of history inevitably confront their ahistoric counterpart...[which grew in the
1990s,] a period so marked by an accelerated present that the past disappeared."[34]

And our final keyword is *impulse*. The Tate archivist Sue Breakell locates the
artists' fascination with archives in the present moment: "Today our lives are
documented in ways unimaginable to previous generations—as seen in recent
debates about information security, both that held by government and that which
we offer up ourselves on such sites as Facebook, tagging our pages and creating
our own taxonomies."[35] This constant auto-historicizing has been cast in a new
light in the era of Artificial Intelligence mining publicly shared content with its
own preservation concerns, exceeding what can be addressed here.

Some artists are concerned with the institutional claims on universality, totality,
and integrity found in collections, but as historian Hal Foster explores in his essay
"The Archival Impulse"—this is assumed but not proclaimed. The orientation is
often more generous than critical, and it often results in artists producing their
own archives. They arrange materials using a quasi-archival logic that includes
the aesthetics of citation, juxtaposition, and so on. He continues to say that rather
than cynicism found in art that critiques institutions, "these artists often aim
to fashion distracted viewers into engaged discussants—here there is nothing
passive about the word 'archival'."[36]

And so without further ado, I want to share ten artist projects with you that
demonstrate this impulse in rough chronology over the last four decades:

In 1983 Martha Minujín, an Argentine artist, made "The Parthenon of Books,"
a tubular structure where more than 20,000 books were attached with their covers
facing out, fully covering a "temple" structure based on the Parthenon. Minujín
chose books that had been banned during the Argentinian military dictatorship
that lasted from 1976 to 1983. The books were donated by more than thirty-five
publishing houses, which had been keeping many of them in storage thanks to the
coordination of the Argentine Book Chamber. In an interview with an Argentine
curator Victoria Noorthoorn, the project was described as

---

[34] Nato Thompson, *Ahistoric Occasion: Artists Making History* (Mass Moca, 2006), 22.

[35] Breakell, "Perspectives: Negotiating the Archive."

[36] Hal Foster, "An archival impulse," October 110 (2024): 3–22, 5–6.

> *A monument to the restoration of democracy...Minujín's public project was*
> *inaugurated on December 19, 1983, only one week after the restitution of democ-*
> *racy...Rather than a conventional monument, however, her ambitious project was*
> *conceived as a participatory work in a public space...On December 24, 1983,*
> *with the help of two cranes, the structure was leant over to one side, allowing*
> *the public to remove the books. Around 12,000 volumes were distributed among*
> *those present, while the remaining 8,000 or so were later sent to public librar-*
> *ies. Minujín's intention was, as she put it, to "return the work to the public."[37]*

Buenos Aires now has more bookstores per capita than any other major city in
the world.

One of the most iconic examples of this kind of work is artist Fred Wilson's
"Mining The Museum" from 1992. This project, while commissioned by the
nomadic museum, The Contemporary, took place at the Maryland Historical
Society which was founded in 1844 to collect, preserve, and study objects related
to the state's history. This mission included accounts of colonization, slavery, and
abolition, but the museum tended to present this history from a specific viewpoint,
namely that of its white male founding board. It was this worldview that Wilson
aimed to "mine." He did so by spending a significant amount of time with the
collection in an artist residency and then ultimately assembling the museum's
collection in a new and surprising way, deploying various personal and satirical
techniques. Staged during the annual meeting of the American Association of
Museums' annual conference, the project was designed strategically to be impactful for the field and continues to be widely discussed today.[38]

The French artist Jean-Luc Moulène's "Objets de grève" (Strike Objects),
completed in 2000, documents objects made by French factory workers while
they were on strike: bright red shoes, strike maps, political figurines, a frying pan
reading "Justice, Liberty, Employment, Solidarity," to name a few. The objects
he photographed were donated and are now at the Archives nationales du monde
du travail (National Archives of the World of Labour) in Roubaix, France.[39]

The "Library Project" by the art collective Temporary Services took place at
the Harold Washington Library in Chicago, which is the largest municipal, public,

[37] Noorthoor, 2011, quoted in Tate. Marta Minujín, "The Parthenon of Books," *Tate*, 1983, https://www.tate.org.uk/art/artworks/minujin-the-parthenon-of-books-t14343.

[38] Lisa G. Corrin, "Mining the Museum: An Installation Confronting History," in *Reinventing the Museum: The Evolving Conversation on the Paradigm Shift*, ed. G. Anderson (Altamira Press, 2012), 114–122.

[39] Vivian Sky Rehberg, "Art of Work," *Frieze*, September 21, 2016, https://frieze.com/article/art-work.

circulating library in the country.[40] With the "Library Project", Temporary Services added 100 new books and artists projects into the library holdings through a donation. The books included unique artist-made books and zines as well as altered books and books with surprises inside. A favorite of mine was Michael Piazza's "Observed Reading on the Armitage Bus 8:15am 2/15/2001," which just took three books that had been in coincidental temporary proximity and bound them together like a special gift-set that could help one understand a little bit about that bus route, that city, and that moment. Like a good intervention, the library was not told about the gifts they were going to receive when the "Library Project" was delivered to their shelves. But the incredible outcome is that the librarians actually accessioned them into their collection and got really excited about it!

The symposium "Speak, Memory: On Archives and Other Strategies of (Re) activation of Cultural Memory" took place at the Townhouse Gallery in Cairo on October 28–30, 2010. Following this event and inspired by the earlier examples from Latin America and Eastern Europe, the organizers stated that they would create

> the "Archive Map" research project, which seeks to create a growing database of archival collections that contain material relevant to the Middle East's modern and contemporary art history [and] will focus on archival collections (whether state-owned or independent) that are open or accessible (at least seemingly) to the public. We have deliberately decided to exclude private collections from this research to avoid an intensification of the ongoing purchase and export of privately held archives in the Middle East.[41]

Jenny Odell's "The Bureau of Suspended Objects" began in 2015 as an artist residency at the Recology SF, the city's resource recovery plant. During the span of the residency Odell archived 200 objects for an exhibition in September 2015. An accompanying Tumblr page included entries for each object with details on its original manufacture, and an accompanying phone app could be used to see images of the original object alongside the recovered one on display in the gallery. The project's stated goals included to "show how the moment of 'becoming trash' has more to do with changing circumstances and emotions than with the material reality of the object."[42]

---

[40] Temporary Services, "The Library Project," 2001, http://www.temporaryservices.org/library_project.pdf.

[41] "Next Steps: The Archive Map," p. 94. Editor Laura Carderera, From Speak Memory: On Archives and Other Strategies of (Re)activation of Cultural Memory, 2010, https://www.academia.edu/20315284/South_South_Intersections_Southern_Conceptualisms_Network_and_the_political_possibilities_of_local_histories.

[42] Jenny Odell, "The Bureau of Suspended Objects," n.d., https://www.suspended-objects.org/about-bso.

In 2015 Theater Gates' Rebuild Foundation organization opened the Stony Island Arts Bank to house several of his collections including: Johnson Publishing Archive + Collections: books and periodicals donated by the Johnson Publishing Company, publisher of "Ebony" and "Jet" magazine; University of Chicago Glass Lantern Slides: over 60,000 slides of art and architectural history from the Paleolithic to Modern eras; the Edward J. Williams Collection: 4,000 objects of "negrobilia"—mass cultural objects and artifacts that feature stereotypical images of black people; and Frankie Knuckles Records: "Godfather of House Music," Frankie Knuckles' vinyl collection. At another Rebuild Foundation site Gates houses the salvaged inventories of the Dr. Wax record store and the remaining architecture and design collection of the long running Prairie Avenue Books—in both cases, the inventory remaining after the going-out-of-business clearance sales. Most recently, the Rebuild Foundation acquired the Dinh Nguyen Collection, an archive of music that holds over 14,000 records collected by a French Vietnamese DJ from Réunion Island. By rehousing these commercial, pop-cultural, and scholarly collections within an independent artist-led institution the work is charged with an artist-centricity rather than being simply an archive that is accessible to artists.

Alejandro Acierto is an artist and musician based in Detroit who has become particularly interested in the historic ephemera related to the colonization and decolonization of the Philippines. In his ongoing project "Revising an abject reliquary," which started in 2017, he has been buying, modifying, and reselling postcards on eBay. The postcards were made from 1912 to 1936, during the period of the Insular government. In the artist's writing he describes this process

in which made objects…are put back into the marketplace for collectors and hobbyists to consume. While this work will ultimately be subject to the same ebb and flow of the auction site, the goal is to ostensibly mythologize the accuracy of any of the objects. By recalibrating eBay as its own type of Archive that is much more malleable than those housed within Institutions, I am attempting to enable formations of resistance within an archive…Through these particular forms of interjection, my intent through all of these works are to actively reconstruct the possibility of my own history and effectively reclaim that which has been lost so as to imagine a decolonized future.[43]

---

[43] Alejandro T. Acierto, "Recalibrating the Archive: Insurgent Acts and Strategies of Renewal" (Presented at the College Art Association in 2018 on the panel "Evasive Articulations in the Age of 'Fake News': Thinking about the Relationship between Art and Truth during the Trump Era." Unpublished paper draft shared with the author.)

Red Conceptualismos del Sur/RedCSur (or the Southern Conceptualisms Network) is a network concerned with the generation of new conditions for the discussion and preservation of artistic and political micro-history materials and documents in their own contexts from across Latin America. As they explain, "Rather than treat them as mere 'sources' of 'the history of art', we envisioned them as living antagonistic forces, capable of intervening in our local memories, our academic apparatuses, and our public debates."[44] The group has staged events and provided theorization, contextualization, and support for a network of local archives. Another fundamental focus has been to confront "disputes over memory" in Latin America, which have sought to censor and manage truth-telling about life in the region since the 1960s.[45] Out of this work have emerged projects focused around archival policies such as the 2019 Call for a Common Archives Policy in the region and several curatorial projects presenting exhibits of poorly represented and documented regional art histories.

Departing in many ways from earlier examples, the Santa Cruz-based artist Laurie Palmer created the project and the 2023 book *The Lichen Museum*, which turns the museum inside out by not being oriented around collecting but redirecting the viewers' attention at the world. As Palmer describes it,

> *Conventions for viewing art in museums establish a safe distance between the viewer and the art as well as protocols for where to stand and how to look, with subject and object positions intact. Observational methods of natural history are also based in a relation of subject to object, observer to observed. We assume that this kind of relation is fundamental to the act of seeing. However, its non-reciprocal distribution of power supports and aligns with the core violence of Western humanism—which transforms whatever is considered not human into less-than-human, into a thing, or a resource, and eventually, a commodity. This mode of relation structures racial catpialism's attempts to capture and possess life, earth and time, and to abuse matter and its energies. It has already rendered parts of the earth unlivable for many, and is proceeding to wreck the rest of it.*[46]

As part of activating the museum, Palmer leads walks in parks and neighborhoods to see where lichen, which are hybrid forms of algae and bacteria, are living and growing all around us every day. The Lichen Museum is everywhere!

---

[44] Joaquín Barriendos, Miguel A. Lopez, and Jaime Vindel, "Micropolitics of the Archive | Part I: Southern Conceptualisms Network and the Political Possibilities of Microhistories," *Asia Art Archive*, December 1, 2012, https://aaa.org.hk/en/ideas/ideas/micropolitics-of-the-archive-part-i-southern-conceptualisms-network-and-the-political-possibilities-of-microhistories.

[45] "Constituent Declaration," *Red Conceptualismos Del Sur*, n.d., https://redcsur.net/manifiesto/#quienessomos.

[46] A. Laurie Palmer, *The Lichen Museum* (University of Minnesota Press, 2023), 5.

Considering the implications of these examples—I am left with three outstanding questions that are inspired by three scholars invested in this kind of work.

First, I am reminded of an interview I heard on NPR years ago, with the historian Nell Irvin Painter reflecting on her experience of becoming an artist later in life after a career as a scholar. She spoke of the difference between being a historian and an artist, reflecting that as an artist "I can do whatever I want with history. As a historian, I had to be faithful to the archive."[47] In this instance, she found this freeing—but I was left wondering what are the implications of this disloyalty to the archive?

Artist Renee Green posed similar concerns after years of making projects dealing with collections and archives. She explained in "Art in America" magazine that

> *even though I read voraciously and use archives, I'd like to move away from a fixation on "the archive," which has been fetishized. Even when you find something interesting, if you don't know what it is, it becomes just kind of quirky. What makes an archive valuable is that you can discover things and understand them in a context. Scholarly knowledge is the ability to recognize something and make associations, creating a deeper understanding. It's easy to be excited by lots of stuff, but it doesn't really mean much without that understanding.*[48]

How can the discourse around multiple ways of knowing, including artistic knowledge, be reconciled with Green's provocation that scholarly research is essential to understanding the context of historical materials?[49]

And a final question to consider about this kind of artwork drawing from another scholar is concerned with how several of the examples above seem as if they are reacting against virtuality by focusing on the tactility of the archival materials. And yet, author Amelia Jones asks us to go deeper to the source to think about the body in relation to archival documentation. She argues that for performance, the archive of the work often lies in the body of the performer. In her writing, she argues for immediacy as she channels French artist Antonin Artaud who wrote in 1938 that the stage should be abolished to reestablish a "direct communication" between "the spectator and the spectacle, between the

---

[47] Scott Simon, "'Old in Art School': An MFA Inspires a Memoir of Age," *NPR*, June 16, 2018, https://www.npr.org/transcripts/620105093.

[48] William S. Smith, "In the Studio: Renée Green," *ARTnews.Com*, June 7, 2022, https://www.artinamericamagazine.com/news-features/magazines/in-the-studio-renee-green.

[49] Elissa Sloane Perry and Aja Couchois Duncan, "Multiple Ways of Knowing: Expanding How We Know," *Non Profit News | Nonprofit Quarterly*, August 12, 2024, https://nonprofitquarterly.org/multiple-ways-knowing-expanding-know/.

actor and the spectator."[50] And with that provocation in mind, I wonder if the examples cited above may require a responsibility to locate embodied histories outside of the objects we leave behind? And what implications does a focus on truly living history have for future archives?

The examples outlined above offer a rich selection of a broader field of practice, in which many diverse practitioners intersecting with, but not limited to, artists have sought to disrupt and experiment with collecting institutions—and in the process to rethink how knowledge and history are categorized, remembered, and preserved. These examples leave many outstanding questions that intersect precisely with the concerns of the Library Company's "Beyond Glass Cases" project, which will be taken up in the conclusion.

Conclusion

In their successful 2022 grant application to the Philadelphia arts foundation, The Pew Center for Arts & Heritage, the Library Company's administrative leadership at the time wrote that

> *"Beyond Glass Cases" is an initiative designed to drive adaptation of the Library Company's exhibitions program and its capacity to engage a broad and diverse audience in the exploration and ever-evolving interpretation of its collections. The project will include an intensive planning phase led by an advisory board composed of a diverse group of cultural heritage thought leaders. The next phase will present three collections-based, public-facing "experiments" centered around controversial items acquired by the Library Company over the course of its ... history.*

The application goes on to ask

> *How does a three hundred year-old institution adapt? "Beyond Glass Cases" (BGC) is designed to drive our adaptation. It is part of an effort to think boldly and honestly about strategies for public engagement with difficult, at times even harmful, collection items. As we approach our 300th birthday in 2031, the Library*

---

[50] Amelia Jones, "'Presence' in Absentia," *Art Journal* 56, no. 4 (December 1, 1997): 11–18, https://doi.org/10. 1080/00043249.1997.10791844.

Company's most pressing challenge is to come to honest terms with its own history.
BGC will present uncomfortable parts of that history within its collections.[51]

And while the transcripts in the following sections will give you a sense of some of the different takes on these exhibition goals, when reading it again today—I am struck by the overall worthiness of these stated ambitions. I am also struck that the project has in it the seeds for addressing these ambitions to adapt. The three "collections lab" experiments were executed critically and creatively by three artists and a collaborating scholar: Tafari Robertson, Mark Thomas Gibson, and Zachariah Julian working with anthropologist and historian Paul Wolff Mitchell. The three projects were skillfully managed by staff liaisons and project managers, all of whom brought their deep knowledge and abiding commitment to the Library Company into their work with these external collaborators.

Later on in the grant application, the authors identify three controversial holdings that warrant further examination. Those include a depiction of T.D. Rice, known as the "father of American minstrelsy," one example of many found in the graphic materials in the Library Company's African American history collection; the painting "Liberty Displaying the Arts and the Sciences" by Samuel Jennings and a bust of Declaration of Independence signer Benjamin Rush which is explained as problematic because "this sculpture is situated prominently amongst a collection of busts of white male figures that gaze down on visitors upon first entering the library. They currently send a clear message about who and what is prioritized." He was described in the grant as "Though an ardent abolitionist, Rush has a controversial legacy that linked Blackness to disease and included disturbing experiments conducted on Black people." And finally, materials from the George Morton Papers were identified as necessitating digitization so that an exhibition could be developed exploring the legacy of what the finding aid suggests were his "craniometric studies of humans with conclusions regarding the relative intellectual capacities of the 'five races'."

Though the projects in the final series of experiments did not explicitly focus on the graphic materials like the depiction of T.D. Rice, the "Black Historians' Department" installation by Tafari Robertson did include some of the materials from the African American history collection. The Jennings painting was a direct prompt and inspiration for Mark Thomas Gibson's paintings and accompanying focus group project; and the installation by Zachariah Julian and Paul Wolff

---

[51]. "The Library Company of Philadelphia Exhibitions & Public Interpretation 2022 Project Grant." Pew Center for Arts & Heritage, 2022. Draft shared with the author.

Mitchell ended up dealing largely with the legacy of Morton and included a decision in collaboration with their staff liaison Rachel D'Agostino, Curator of Printed Books, to turn the bust of Rush and others to face the wall while visitors entered the exhibit.

And still, despite successfully executing these ambitious projects, there was a sense in many of my conversations around this project that the process had been compromised and messy. People cited staff turnover and leadership transitions, tight organizational finances, being enticed by grants with demands that exceed capacity, and a concern that the lessons might not be incorporated back into the institution or the partnerships not maintained following the project completion. That the worthy goals were compromised by dynamics prevalent in the entire field makes these issues relevant to the entire field. At a moment when there is a larger war on public memory, a project like "Beyond Glass Cases" is caught between the ethical tensions internal to the Library Company of Philadelphia and the larger political context. The ways in which a particular organization experiences budgetary woes and turnover are not separable from the economic pressures impacting scarcity in nonprofit resources, changes in the labor market, and the weaponization of various tools of cultural policy. While this publication may focus more on the micro-internal forces, these macro-external forces at work should not be forgotten.

Following my interview with Shannon Mattern in this section which seeks to give greater context to the "Beyond Glass Cases" project, the rest of the two sections in this book focus on the voices of the people who made the exhibits and events happen. The people interviewed in the following two sections will at times share contradictory views of the same event. There are also people mentioned (former staff, leaders, and consultants) who do not get to represent themselves, but who, taken in good faith, were committed to advancing the Library Company of Philadelphia as an institution through critical interrogation of its past. As with any moment in time, some aspects of the organizational trajectory will have to be determined and owned by those dedicated staffers and institutional leaders who are at the helm today.

Section 2 delves into the creative contributors of the three projects that took place. There are photo portfolios of the work and extensive interviews with Mark Thomas Gibson, Tafari Robertson, Zachariah Julian, and Paul Wolff Mitchell. They discuss the process through which they came to "Beyond Glass Cases" and what they ultimately made in response to the opportunity. Each conversation gives insight into the creative process that these partners brought to the Library Company.

Section 3 highlights the voices of Library Company staff members, advisory board members, and anonymous hotline respondents. These interviews give a look behind the curtain that reveal how projects like "Beyond Glass Cases" are made and administered, who makes them happen, and what concerns arise in the process.

Building on 294 years of history, the document of a three-year initiative that you have in your hands will hopefully be useful and instructive. If anything, it takes that dramatic gap in time and pushes it together. As a project aspiring to ask "How does a three hundred year-old institution adapt?," the answer cannot be found in the commitments of any one time period. As the Library Company looks forward—the voices brought together here can offer insight about what to do, what not to do, and the stakes for adaptation.

Interview: Shannon Mattern

In order to extend some of the themes of the introductory essay and explore "Beyond Glass Cases" in relation to the library field more generally, this interview brings in the voice of the library scholar and educator Shannon Mattern

This interview was conducted by Daniel Tucker on August 7, 2025.

Daniel: So you've talked about how in your first book, "The New Downtown Library," which was about library architecture among other topics, how the book ended up being sought out by library staff. And I'm imagining that that was significant also because it was an academic book in its initial conception. I'm wondering if you could talk a little bit about how you settled on that topic for the book and then how releasing it and that experience of who was drawn to it ended up changing your relationship to the field?

Shannon: I ended up in a PhD program in Media Studies, and I happened to land in New York University. It was the first time I lived in a big city, and I was impressed by the intense physical materiality of the city. The city itself as a communication medium really struck me. Seeing the vibrance of the library systems around the city also made me want to find a case study for my dissertation that combined a lot of my interests, as the libraries did.

And it just so happened that the Seattle Public Library was being designed at that time. So I followed that specific project, which is a really interesting case study that allowed me to ask questions about how a city manifests its identity in physical form and aesthetics, how we manage the transition [between] or the balance the analog and digital, how we take a public space and make it accountable and responsible to different stakeholders and community groups? So this integration of public process and public aesthetics and civic values were all integrated into that case study. And then I got a grant to go around the country to fifteen cities where, despite the fact that lots of folks predicted that a new company called Amazon was going to render the library obsolete, many cities were still building new and ambitious downtown libraries because they regarded it as a vital, vibrant, and necessary institution that communicated a city's commitment to public knowledge.

Daniel: And so just kind of picking up on that, I'm wondering if you could talk a little bit about releasing it and the reception that you got, how that kind of changed your relationship to the field over the course of many years?

Shannon: The book was originally under contract with Smithsonian Books, whose ethos seemed very appropriate for the book's subject matter. But then the press underwent some sort of restructuring—even as my book was *in press*—so I had to find a new publisher, then pass through peer review and editing all over again. Thus, there was a lot of tension and a bit of resentment and exhaustion around the book. So I really had minimal hopes for its reception. I was just glad to get it out there…But it just so happened that library directors and library architects around the country indicated that they found it useful: it addressed the larger thematic and critical issues that were germane to these types of projects, but then translated them into a concrete design process that they found accessible and useful. I just visited folks in the DC public library recently, and the library director pulled my book off the shelf and said, "I still reference this with people." So, that was really rewarding to know that my interlocutors, the "subjects" of my book, actually found it useful. I wasn't just writing about them, I was writing for them, too.

Afterward, I received a number of invitations to work with design organizations, to consult on design projects. Those doors opened up, I think, when people realized that I really took to heart and did justice to the knowledge of librarians and designers and all the people involved in library design. So lots of practical partnerships and collaborations became possible after that book came out.

Daniel: Then you continued to write about libraries and near the time the book came out, you started writing for *Places* journal, and you wrote a piece called "Marginalia: Little Libraries in the Urban Margins." Can you summarize what you learned about little libraries at that time and then how you saw that kind of work evolving over the last fifteen years, especially in light of some of the observations that you made in your later piece "Fugitive Libraries"?

Shannon: Another one of my motivations to study libraries is that there had been so much theorizing about the archive when I was in graduate school, often in ways that did not engage at all with the professional literature and practice of archivists. It was thinking about the archive as metaphor or as aesthetic or as a poetic idea, which, sure—there's value to that, but many practicing archivists were rightly frustrated that people weren't engaging with their own field's scholarship. I was struck by the fact that libraries are just as political, just as ethically charged, just as vital and essential institutions as archives, but they weren't being theorized in the same way.

I was also noticing that the library had been a theme, a topic, an aesthetic reference in many of the art exhibitions I was seeing. Experimental magazines

were doing little pop-up libraries in various exhibitions, libraries inspired
the form of countless shows, many exhibitions included reading rooms into
the galleries proper. I was just wondering about the resonance of the library
as an aesthetic form? Why was it appearing so frequently in the art world?

At the same time, we saw the prevalence of these "little free libraries"
[giving away books] and little pop-up book collections, not just in stoop sales,
but in more formally designed architectural installations. I was wondering:
what was happening in the world that generated or incited these kinds of
converging phenomena? I saw that many of these interventionist projects
were responding to the hyper-commercialization of the public sphere;
threats posed to libraries (which have only amplified in recent years); the
hyper-commercialization of publishing; and people's exhaustion with the
digital realm. Some people missed the physical transfer of materials, the touch
of information. I saw a desire to claim space in a hyper-commercialized,
gentrified public realm for the free exchange of material knowledge.

I also wanted to address some concerns that urban planners or city admin-
istrators might see such "crowdsourced" projects and think, "Oh we don't
really need to support the official public institution because communities
will organize their own mutual-aid exchanges." I sought to understand how
the informal, the guerilla, tactical urbanism could partner in a productive
way with official institutions—not parasitic or cannibalistic, but symbiotic.

Daniel: And then you later deepened this inquiry with your piece on "Fugutive
    Libraries", and I'm just wondering if you could share a little bit about how
    that maybe represented an evolution in your thinking about the field?

Shannon: I'll admit that some academic work is driven by annoyance or spite. In
    some cases, you get so tired of popular "takes" or public misunderstandings
    that you feel compelled to stage a rebuttal. A particular trade book came out
    in 2018 that was celebrating the library as a do-it-all social infrastructure—a
    romantic celebration of libraries as the one remaining totally accessible, fully
    democratic public space that has also valiantly taken on all these other social
    roles. It offers afterschool programs, it offers elder care, it is a mental health
    facility—so celebrate our hero librarians because they are doing it all, and they
    somehow find a way to fit all of this into their modest budgets and on their modest
    salaries. That book got a lot of traction, and I found myself involved in a lot of
    workshops and conferences that were inspired by that book—despite the fact
    that it didn't seem to find inspiration in, or engage with, relevant prior research.

    After yet another event where the participants were speaking rhapsodically
    about the library as an embodiment of inclusive democracy I thought to

myself, yet again: this is not the case—not everybody is welcome in a library. We still have issues of exclusion, problems of inaccessibility, legacies of colonial systems. So, I was prompted to write "Fugitive Libraries," which was an extension of my previous piece about pop-up guerilla, experimental collections. Fugitive libraries, unlike many of these others, were often created out of necessity.

This new research also allowed me to engage with the deeper history of racial segregation in knowledge institutions. In many cases, communities [that] found themselves not welcomed or not represented in the official public institution, have had to or chosen to create their own collections that more closely align with their values—that politics of self-identification. So I aimed to engage with this longer, deeper history of exclusion, and trace it through contemporary practices of improvisation and experimentation by marginalized communities. I also wanted to be sure that I wasn't claiming ownership of these ideas, so I focused on interviews and prioritized the words of the fugitive librarians themselves. I wanted to use that piece to highlight their work, not to claim some kind of theoretical intervention of my own.

Daniel: You started to touch on this popular notion of libraries doing everything, being these kinds of catchall spaces. And I know that you've written in your essay "Library as Infrastructure" about the increasing number of functions that are expected of libraries in other places, but it reminded me of something that a friend who's a librarian at the Free Library of Philadelphia, Adam Feldman, who told me about metrics at the Free Library. Essentially, he was saying that, according to all the classic metrics that they are evaluated by like books being checked out, things are going downhill. People are not checking out as many books (not counting eBooks and the kind of explosion of libraries making those accessible). But what had really shifted in terms of metrics was event attendance going way up. And so increasingly, every librarian was expected to do programming in their space, whether they were doing lap story hours with infants or programming with the Philadelphia Jazz Project to do a residency playing sheet music in the music collection. Both the neighborhood branches and the main branch of the Philadelphia Free Library were just brimming with events. And so one of the things that struck me in that description was that the job of the librarian had dramatically changed what they were trained to do in terms of library science and was not necessarily reflecting this new culture of programming and events. And so I was wondering if you could talk a little bit about this tension between the historical functions of libraries and these newer expectations, the way in which that's changing the division of labor and the culture within the spaces?

Shannon: This expanding purview of librarianship extends far beyond activating the collection through events and programming and reading groups and workshops and labs, et cetera. The expansion encompasses myriad social infrastructural dimensions, too, because of a failing social safety net. One of the major questions of my 2014 "Library as Infrastructure" article was how elastic the library's mission can be? How far can we expect this institution and the people who work in it to stretch themselves to be social workers and surrogate parents and elder care workers, and to liaise with the police and immigration officials, et cetera. So the extension of the job is a much larger and broader challenge. But with regard to your specific question about programming: this is something that I think librarians have different thoughts about.

Some librarians I know really enjoy finding ways to take their collections and share them in multiple formats, to make exhibitions out of them, to share their own excitement about the material through activating or performing the collection and new modalities. And I think that might be in part because most of my friends are hybrid librarians/artists who have these two sets of interests and impulses, and they love to think about how they can inform one another. But to Adam's point, this is indeed an additional skillset that's required on the job, but which isn't often developed in training. It involves event planning, it involves program management, all types of managerial and logistical work and other sets of skills that aren't necessarily covered in library school. There are varying degrees of institutional support for this type of work, too. Events require the involvement of communications, facilities, security, and A/V staff.

Daniel: In my interview with the staff liaisons at the Library Company who worked on this "Beyond Glass Cases" project, one of them commented that they had all been out of school for fifteen years or more, and that they had not necessarily received training to do the essentially curatorial and community engagement work that they were being asked to do. And so we talked a little bit about, well, what would that training look like? There's a version of it that is more focused on community engagement. There's a version of it that's more focused on curatorial practice, but probably there's not a version that does everything that might come up in these situations. I'm curious what things you've heard about the evolution of this conversation in terms of library education?

Shannon: I haven't traced that genealogy; that would require looking back through the evolution of MLIS curricula. Perhaps someone has already done this work, but I haven't encountered it. The different ways of activating and facilitating those connections, getting books into people's hands—these are extensions of long-standing reader services. But the different modalities of activation and outreach have indeed proliferated.

    Some better-resourced libraries do have librarians dedicated specifically to community engagement. Some libraries have events and exhibitions teams who can help with much of this work. Having such support systems could make curation and community engagement feel like exciting opportunities. If the responsibility falls on a skeleton staff, in which everyone has to be a jack of all trades, these opportunities could feel more like a burdensome obligation.

Daniel: I'm wondering how some of these things that we're talking about are going to sort of manifest in this curriculum that you are designing right now? So recently you've taken on this role as the Director of Creative Research at the Metropolitan New York Library Council (METRO), and you're launching something called the Cross-Reference Coalition where people can convene in a kind of free school to grow and learn together. I'm just wondering if you could talk a little bit about what taking on this role has made you think about—regarding what the library field needs in terms of training, learning in community and professional or peer education?

Shannon: The library field has a lot of needs—and is facing many compounding challenges—that I can't presume to address. Book bans, cuts to funding, conservatives' disbelief in public goods, threats to and attacks on librarians from folks threatened by challenging ideas. Higher education is facing many of its own challenges, including an egregious inability to address purportedly "controversial" issues like gender identity and racial inclusion and ideological diversity. And universities' utter failure to stand up for the values spelled out in their mission statements has rendered them vulnerable to internal sabotage, by obstructionist trustees and alums, and to extortion by the Trump regime. These and other institutional failures have compelled me to leave higher education after 25 years of service, after climbing to the top of the mountain. I feel like my own personal values and commitments—and the needs of this particular political moment—have pulled me toward libraries, which, as we've discussed, have been a subject of my research and teaching, and frequent partners, throughout my career. I had also served for ten years on the board of the Metropolitan New York

Library Council (METRO), which allowed me to think across its several hundred member institutions, representing myriad species of knowledge institutions. This just feels like a space of greater civic vitality and necessity and possibility—one that's more aligned with the commitments that require valiant defense today. Hence my decision to make an institutional and career shift: I've left a full, tenured, presidential professorship to become the Director of Creative Research at the METRO.

And then in terms of the Cross-Reference Coalition, which is just one of the projects that I'll be germinating as I grow into this new role: it's an opportunity for me to build on skills and interests I've developed throughout my career—I'll be developing exuberantly interdisciplinary classes, that celebrate the collections and services of our member institutions, and that welcome into our learning cohort the knowledge workers and graduate students from our member institutions, accompanied by artists and designers. So, this new work is in part a means of sustaining and activating my own skills and interests, but making them useful to the cultural heritage workers and institutions of New York.

There are plenty of professional education opportunities [in the field], but we are not that. As I've put it in our planning documents, the Cross-Reference Coalition is an experimental learning community dedicated to discovering what new knowledges and creative practices might emerge through integrative thinking, through interdisciplinary collaborations, through inter-institutional partnerships, through the activation of New York City's shared public knowledge.

Daniel: And I'm sure the range of organizations and institutions that you'll interface with have a wide range of resource situations as well in terms of what they might even have accessible to them in terms of training.

Shannon: Yes, absolutely. One of the things I love about METRO is that it functions, in part, as a sort of integrative infrastructure, or a "commons" between other institutions. It prioritizes the sharing of resources and knowledge among the big and the small, the rich and the poor. Our member institutions range from the New York, Brooklyn, and Queens public libraries to the university and hospital and museum libraries, to small community archives. METRO exists to knit these people together, to allow them to reap the network effects, to be greater than the sum of their parts.

Daniel: In the final phase of the Library Company's "Beyond Glass Cases" project they engaged in a collaboration with Rowhome Productions to create a hotline to collect feedback about their project and ask questions that were

pertinent to the field more broadly as well as the Library Company specifically. One of the questions asked "Should libraries and museums strive to
strike a balance in displaying collections that tell both positive and critical
stories about history? Should controversial or offensive items ever be placed
on public display, or should they be brought out only by specific request?"
Obviously that is a rich question and I am sure one that you have a take
on, but I wanted to share one of the anonymous responses that struck me:

> *I do think that in the right context, you can display controversial or offensive*
> *items as long as they're explained in the right way. Libraries are not museums,*
> *so it's really hard to put those kinds of things into context. I think it's easier if*
> *you are a museum because that is part of your job.*

Based on your experience and research, can you reflect on that distinction
that this audience member is making? Do you think the job of the museum
and library are crucially different?

Shannon: The GLAM sector encompasses galleries, libraries, archives, and
museums. There are ontological and epistemological differences between
these different institutional types, but there's also a lot of vitalizing bleed
between them. And as their individual purviews expand, as we were talking
about earlier, we find little seeds of each institutional type in all the others.
You're talking about libraries creating exhibitions, incorporating exhibition spaces themselves. Many libraries have archives within themselves.
Museums have their own libraries. Especially when you have this nesting
doll, or Venn diagram, configuration, we can ask questions about where
the boundaries lie between these institutional species, or whether those
boundaries are productively porous. And there are generative things they
can learn from one another too: what does it mean to prioritize discovery,
to think capaciously about provenance, to think experimentally about display, to think about different conceptions of "value." And we can maybe
think about GLAM as a terrain of overlapping zones, to think about their
common purposes.

Now, to the hotline commenter's point—that libraries don't have the same
critical framing that museums do: If you have all of your material on open
shelves, and you allow folks to pull any book off the shelf without intervention or contact with a staff member or a pedagogical framing experience
or an orientation to the institution, a visitor could experience a shocking or
traumatizing encounter with a "controversial" object. Sometimes you can

place certain materials—for instance, those, engaging with sensitive topics like genocide or including adult imagery—into restricted access areas. Especially with the rise of book bans, many libraries are forced to take items addressing particular subject matter and place them into restricted access zones. The intention is that a child or teen would then have to ask permission to access a book about gender identity or racism, for instance. This raises all kinds of questions about who gets to determine what constitutes a "controversial" subject. Controversial to whom? In what context? The facts that all human beings deserve to have dignity, that the United States has a deep legacy of slavery: to some people, these are actually controversial statements. Inconvenient facts, unsavory histories: these difficult ideas are coded as "controversial" and placed behind a firewall, where the friction and stigma of submitting a special access request will likely keep many readers from ever encountering these ideas. These scenarios raise political and ethical questions about what constitutes a controversial issue.

We see this happening even in Philadelphia [right now], as the Trump administration is considering the removal of exhibitions in Independence National Historical Park that frame the U.S. in a less-than-stellar light. Libraries could take a similar approach: simply removing entire exhibitions, entire collection items, that spark controversy. Yet libraries also have at their disposal a range of options: placing a boundary around a collection to ensure that there is a librarian there to mediate access, adding contextual notes to catalog records.

In an exhibition you have wall texts and program notes and docents and curators, you have multiple layers of contextualization that can prepare people for what they're about to encounter, help them to understand that an institution's choice to exhibit particular material or having a particular item in their collection is not an endorsement of the ideas it presents or the values that it embodies. Instead, we have it because we have to engage with the full fraughtness of our history. This artifact is a part of this sordid story that we're living together. All of those forms of intellectual, pedagogical, aesthetic framing can create a prismatic apparatus for critical interpretation. Perhaps this is where libraries can draw from the traditions of the museum to help to provide that context.

Daniel: The Library Company developed this project, "Beyond Glass Cases", with a few goals in mind that included a focus on some of their controversial objects in their holdings and also exhibition strategies more generally, experimenting with creating different kinds of audience engagement around them, and then also about working with artists to interpret their collection and to activate their spaces. So I'm wondering if you could talk a little bit about some examples that you've seen of other libraries specifically taking on these same goals that the Library Company had set up for "Beyond Glass Cases?"

Shannon: There are, especially since the rise of social justice initiatives, and particularly since 2020, a lot of institutions [that] have engaged with their legacies of colonialism and racism.

Daniel: Are there any that stand out to you as exemplary?

Shannon: My friend Dorothy Berry, who is now the digital curator at the National Museum of African American History and Culture in DC, spent several years at Harvard digitizing and curating collection materials pertaining to slavery, abolition, and emancipation.

We can also look to something that public libraries have done for a very long time: developing exhibitions during Banned Book Week. They'll find creative ways to exhibit banned books and then often host programming to encourage different age groups to engage with those materials—and with the whole concept of censorship. There's lots of sensitivity that has to be implemented in discussing these issues.

We can also look to activist collections that have explicit progressive missions, whose very existence might be "controversial" to some folks.

Daniel: And then in terms of some of the other goals of the Library Company, they are also thinking about experimenting with exhibition strategies and working with artists to interpret the collection. I know there's a lot of examples of this, but I'm wondering if there's any that particularly stand out to you of these experiments with exhibition making?

Shannon: I think that the New York and Brooklyn Public Libraries have a really long legacy of engaging with artists representing different artistic traditions, to activate, to ask critical questions about the material. Dancers, improv theater, composers, social practice artists. These different modalities resonate with people in different ways, which might prompt questions that a sterilized clinical presentation in a vitrine might not.

One archival artist I really admire, who engages with controversial issues in sensitive and provocative ways, is Stephanie Syjuco. She works with photographs and other representations of racist, colonial histories. In her "Block Out the Sun" series, which I've written about elsewhere, she uses her own hands to block out photos of Filipinos taken at the St. Louis World's Fair. The use of her own hands as a redaction tool prompts us to ask questions about the subjectivity of the researcher and what we're allowed, or now allowed, to see. What are our ethical obligations to depicted subjects? What are the politics of obfuscation and redaction? Do we have the authority to speak on behalf of archival subjects? Such work can prompt very valuable methodological and ethical questions.

I'm also thinking of Theaster Gates, who, by reviving and recontextualizing discarded artifacts of Black history, and by displaying those materials in different furniture assemblages or activating them through song, can prompt forms of discussion and embodied engagement that a more traditional clinical display wouldn't be able to.

Daniel: In the essay, I'm writing for this book I look at artists doing this kind of work, including Gates, and then I conclude that section with some more contrarian or critical examples. And one is the historian Nell Irvin Painter, who then has pursued a practice as a visual artist after retirement. And she talked about reflecting on her experience as a scholar versus an artist and how she engages with archives differently. And she says that as an artist, she can do whatever she wants with history…But as a historian, she had to be faithful to the archive. And then I also look at Renee Green, who has done a bunch of these kinds of projects in the past, but she ended up sharing in an interview that she rethought that practice a little bit, and she says,

> *I'd like to move away from a fixation on the archive. Even when you find something interesting, if you don't know what it is, it becomes just kind of quirky. What makes an archive valuable is that you can discover things and understand them in context. Scholarly knowledge is the ability to recognize something and make associations and create deeper understanding.*

So these two examples are sort of on my mind right now in terms of thinking about what can artists learn from librarians?

Shannon: Absolutely. I'm glad you're asking that question. I think people like Nell Painter and Renee Green [are posing these concerns] because they have those dual identities, and because they're trained in the protocols of historical research and engagement with the archive. I really appreciate the work of those artists who engage with librarians and archivists, those who have done some ethnographic work in these institutions and engaged with knowledge workers' professional knowledge; they know the affordances and limitations of these institutions.

SECTION 2

Creative Partners

"Lineage" By Mark Thomas Gibson

October 15, 2024–January 17, 2025

Through four large-scale paintings, Mark Thomas Gibson's "Lineage" examined the proposition of "the future of humanity" proposed by Samuel Jennings' 1792 painting "Liberty Displaying the Arts and Sciences (or The Genius of America Encouraging the Emancipation of the Blacks)." The paintings were informed from Library Company holdings depicting the figure Liberty and listening sessions with Philadelphia high school history teachers; high school students from the social justice media program POPPYN; community leaders attending the political education program Du Bois Movement School for Abolition & Reconstruction; and volunteers from the Paul Robeson House and Museum. The works represent the session participants' envisioned futures for humanity. Gibson's paintings were composed as retellings of historical events within the Western narrative painting tradition and sought to reorient viewers to understand how fictional our perception and relationship is with history and potential outcomes.

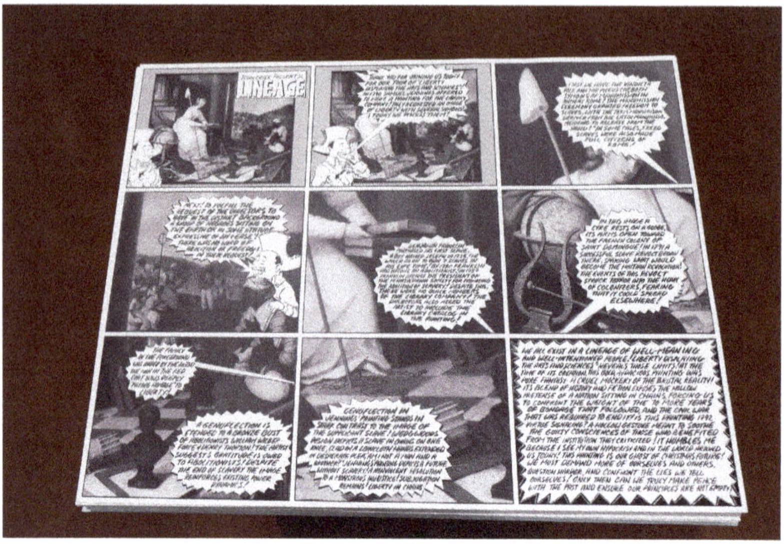
LINEAGE

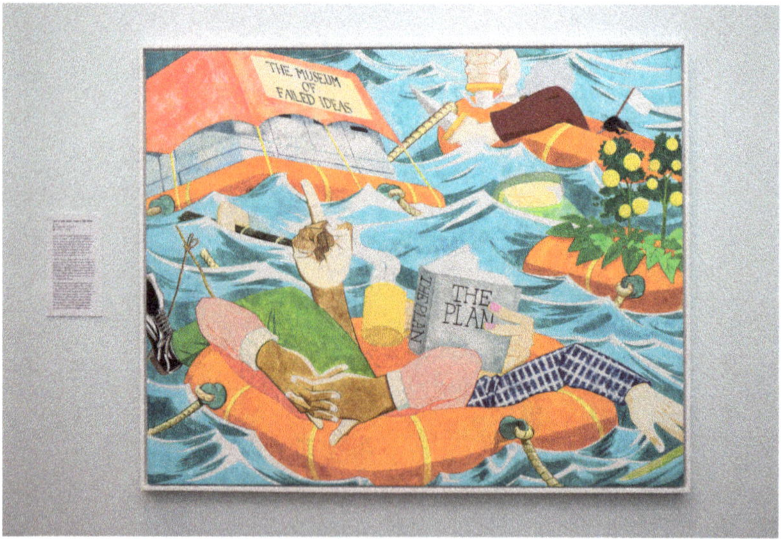
THE MUSEUM OF FAILED IDEAS
THE PLAN

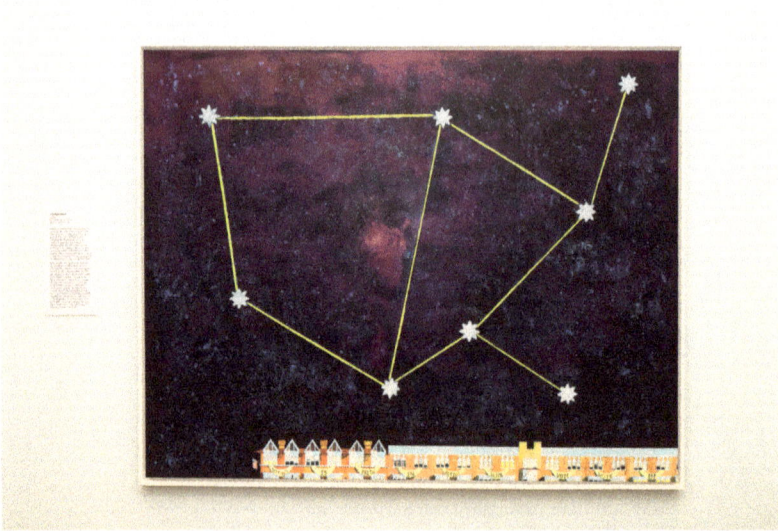

Interview: Mark Thomas Gibson

This interview was conducted by Daniel Tucker on March 24, 2025.

Daniel: I thought it was important before talking about the "Beyond Glass Cases" and "Lineage" work, to just get a little bit of a sense of a prehistory, especially again for readers who are encountering this maybe in the context of the Library Company's work, but might be unfamiliar with your trajectory—to just sort of understand a little bit more about your long-term engagement with American history and politics. I also know that you've been involved with campaigns around voting and one of your pieces that was exhibited at the Library Company even used this kind of slogan that "voting is faith in action." So just wondered if you could talk a little bit about maybe an early experience with politics or political history that led you to decide to center these themes in your artwork.

Mark: I think that my work for many years, it's funny you have your politics and then you don't really think that maybe they bleed into the work that you make. And in 2020 or towards that 2020 election, my work started to take on more of a clear direct opposition to the President at that time. And during that process, my work was noticed by the People for the American Way who had asked me to be a part of an ad campaign. And I usually I prefer to kind of engage with things politically more on my own terms. I don't like to really use my skillset for general use because I feel that it can be misused. I don't always agree fully with the politics of other groups. So I know that I'm very particular. So even in this last election cycle, I kind of was more withholding about my work and what I did and what I produced. And I was reached out to by some organizations to work with them. Basically, I was like, I can't because I don't fully believe in all your politics. It's difficult because given the nature of what we were dealing with, I had to find my own way and make my own peace with it.

The project at the Library Company fits into that, where I was at a crossroads in my own making and realized that I had perhaps become too self-involved, meaning that you can still do work and maybe speak to a politic that is of the people, but are you really listening to the people? And I took the opportunity to reach out to groups and to reach out to organizations to get feedback on what it is that they thought was at stake here and what was actually occurring in the country. So the imagery and the language, even in the work, is so much more generated from the people that I encountered rather than my own politics. In some ways, I had to couch a bit of my politics to do the work, which was frustrating to be honest.

But at the same time, it was illuminating. And in some places, like in the case of the work that you just described, I found myself reengaged with that simple proposition and all the ramifications that come from it. And I think that too often we forget and we have forgotten that there are basic systems that are in play that basically keep the dam in order. When those systems are not practiced properly, the dam explodes. And at this moment, that's what we're dealing with. An explosion in, I don't know, words like oligarchy, tyranny, all these things, they're all occurring at the same time. But I feel like when you make a work like this and you make a body of work like this and you put it into a place with such historical significance, you hope that it can either support, possibly nurture those who also, wherever their political stripes are, maybe more so towards mine, feel like there's possibility to unite, to do something, to come together, to make something occur.

Daniel: Thanks for reflecting a little bit on that history and the current moment as well. I want to work our way back into some of the process that you started to describe in terms of conversations with local organizations and also what you ultimately presented as part of this "Lineage" project at the Library Company. But I thought maybe as a way into it, I wanted to understand a little bit about the origin of your involvement. So as I've gleaned, there's this painting that we're going to talk a fair amount that was made by Samuel Jennings in 1792, "Liberty Displaying the Arts and Sciences or the Genius of America, Encouraging the Emancipation of the Blacks," which has been celebrated by the Library Company, to whom Jennings donated this work, as the first painting done by an American-born artist to address the issue of slavery. But I'm wondering, was that painting the beginning of your involvement in the "Beyond Glass Cases" project?

Mark: I think there had been this call for artists to look at elements of their collection. And I can't remember if it was something where they had a series of things to possibly take a look at or if it was just something that came up in conversation. But it immediately caught my interest and I was latched onto it, given where I was in my own life, the idea that an artist [like Jennings] would decide and reach out to an organization who had supported him, but felt that it was necessary to go to them and say, what do you want? What do you want me to make? How do you see yourselves? What do you want me to articulate for you? And I thought that given where I was in my own politics and at that moment, that offering my services to this organization in a way and kind of taking on certain methods that I normally would never use, that I'd have an opportunity to learn something, I'd have an opportunity to give something back. I'd have an opportunity to engage in communities in Philadelphia. I think often when we talk about community engagement, which was a very heavy, heavily pushed thing, especially much more so I think in Philadelphia than other cities. [I wondered] how could I do that and actually feel like I was actually being genuine about the process as opposed to just doing it as a, "Hey, I'm going to make what I just make and you're going to like it. And I'll say it's for the community."

So the process for me going into it was, I talked to a friend who was a UX designer, and I was like, "Hey, I have a series of questions that I'm thinking about asking people, how do we do something like this?" And so I sat down with him and we went through these questions and we talked about different metrics and different ways and openings and different formations of conversation. We used a moderator, so I did some level of presentation of the works and what the project was, but then I had a moderator who stepped in and kind of did most of the conversation with the group. That way I could be in the room. But…people [would not turn to me to ask] "What do you make? What do you think? What do you want?" I'm like, no, I kind of am outside of it.

Daniel: And so just to clarify with that, so when you had these meetings with these groups, which ranged from high school teachers to community organizers, were you enlisting them to respond to that Samuel Jennings painting? Were you enlisting them to give you ideas about content for paintings that you wanted to make? What were you stating as "the ask" to them?

Mark: There's stages to it. There's the acknowledgment of the Jennings painting that I had where I had it on a projection of it up on a screen. And then I made sure, and this was a major part of it, I'm like "no, you should actually come down to the Library Company because I don't know if you've ever even been here, take this opportunity to know that this thing exists. [And] that's where the painting is." So I would show them the projection, I would give a little bit of history, and then I'd show them the actual painting itself, and so they could actually see its scale and its life and its reality. And then I'd answer whatever questions they maybe had, if it was about glazing, if it was about significance of color, significance of compositions, things like that that I'd researched and thought about with the work.

But then I turned off when we go back to the room or come back to where we were sitting, I would turn off the projection and I would I would try to focus on what was the actual, the conceptual conceit of the project, of what Jennings asked of the Library Company. So that these individuals in this period of time are not simply just living in a space of making remarks back towards the painting. I was like, can we sit in this moment and to truly gather our thoughts and think about what is going on in our country? What is of importance? Where are we going? What is going on in the city and what is of importance and where are we going?

So that kind of idea of this moment and yet projection, because in that Samuel Jennings painting, I see it as a little bit of a science fiction painting. I see it as this kind of element that we can look at it, and we look at it and see if it is as an object of the past. But at that period of time in 1790 some, what is that, seventy years before the actual emancipation occurs, you are looking at an object that's speaking to a future, speaking to the possibility of a future. Even using a fictional, fictitious body as this goddess that's sitting there—we can think of that goddess as a flux capacitor, some type of sci-fi device that allows for entryway into a portal. The idea of an outside space where there's a kind of column that's breaking up the space and kind of creating a sense of an interior and exterior. There's a portal kind of happening there.

These were things that I didn't maybe always delve so heavily into with folks because I think that some of these ideas are concepts for people who don't typically think in these terms. It kind of takes them a little bit to the side. So given the time that I had with individuals, which was an hour, I tried to expedite the process by showing them the work, telling them the conceptual conceit, and then trying to get them to respond. That is difficult because I think there's the generality of common conversation that individuals have when they walk into a space and then they start to talk about politics. And the teachers were much more easy to work with because I think that they operate on that level all the time. The students are a little bit more hesitant because I feel that they were divided between what are the topics that the world's typically comfortable with us discussing, versus what is it that we really want to talk about. So it took a little time for that to edge out. And every group is different. I think that the older group, the Robeson House, they had, this wasn't their first rodeo. And I think for me, knowing that about them and their age group was about how do I negotiate a conversation with individuals who have been asked to offer their thoughts and suggestions probably a billion times at this point? And so the major focus of their conversation was about voting. I just really just sat there and allowed for that conversation to happen.

And that's where the work comes from. In each case, it was like if you're talking to younger people about homophobia and gender rights and abortion and gun violence and Project 2025. These are all things that they said, things that I didn't bring up. So it's like you get in this great game of hearing snippets of things that maybe you are concerned with sprinkled around. But similar to the information that's given into Jennings, there isn't a hard object to object, clear definition with subject and context and all this.

Daniel: Continuing with your process of having these conversations with folks, I guess I want to talk a little bit more about, or hear a little bit about the paintings that resulted and which you gave the title "Lineage." I'm just wanting to hear more about the decision-making in the paintings themselves and how that melded with, as you were saying, texts or references that came up in the conversation versus other decisions that you were making as an artist?

Mark: Yeah. So we recorded the conversations and my process was to sit down, listen to the conversations, and then I would start sketching things out. There were some things that came to me early on that maybe would get tossed away and then come back and I'd revisit and re-sketch. I went to an artist residency in California for six weeks [where I continued working on them]. So some of the paintings were on its way, on its journey. So that kind of became the lodestar to understand everything else that was happening. And then as far as the scale of the paintings, I wanted them to be a one-to-one scale with the actual Jennings paintings themselves. So the scale of the paintings are the same size as the Jennings work. I knew I had to think about the possibility of the concept of landscape and environment when thinking about these works and working narratively with figuration, what does that mean for me?

And in the case of a work-like plan in one hand and hope in the other, there was such a particular dystopic conversation that was occurring there. And climate change had come up in many of the works. So the rainfall in another one of the works has this kind of organic type of texture that I wanted inside of this overgrowth, like a rebirthing of nature. So each one, I tried to sit down and just listen to what the people were saying. And then one of the individuals said, "we should have an archive of failure." And that really stuck out to me because I think that so often and what we're even hearing politically what's going on with this administration is these old ideas and these old practices that are being used as a sense of opposition towards this government. They're not working, and it's this sentiment of you don't recognize your failed ideas and you continue to try to use them, your same lobbyist, your same whomever.

So I think that in some way when making it work like this, I want to create records for myself or create language that I think others could borrow. The idea that there's a person in the boat who's reading a book called "The Plan," this kind of general sort of thing that is like we all are supposedly agreed upon, but yet no one actually understands and defines it and there's one person in with their finger in the air because there's always that contradictory body that's in that space. You have the one person who's just kind of leaning back in the raft just taking it on, and there's another hand. I originally wanted to have a hand that was reaching out towards an oar that had kind of got away from them. Then the back is the saboteur, the person who's a part of the group and inside of the community, but it's also destroying it from the inside and trying to make us forget the failed ideas. At the same time there's all of these little games that I'm thinking about once the setting is created, but these are all kind of born out of things that I'm experiencing in the conversation, even with the group of people sitting in front of me and that's the fun of it.

For me, in the case of the constellation piece, I've never made a painting like that before. It is just a strange painting for me. And I'm sitting there and I'm drawing, and I think originally it was supposed to be a street scene with poles, maybe having a light post in the foreground, kind of a North Philly street scene and wiring and everything else like that, and intermixing, that would be "vote" things everywhere and people coming in and handing out ballots and talking. And then it was sort of becoming this very phony, almost kind of 1980s afterschool special type of energy, that was so candy-coated and plastic that it felt like it was cynical and it felt like it was going to be… it would be nasty. And as I'm drawing it, and I mean I sketch the whole thing out, and I had it laid out and stoops and everything else, and potted plants. I mean, I had this whole world laid out and I was just like, "what the hell is this? What is this?"

Daniel: But can I ask, is that a familiar kind of juncture that you find yourself in your work, or do you believe that that actually came from this kind of unusual process that you subjected yourself to?

Mark: I think it came from the process. I think it came from the process of trying to figure out what is my duty to please others in this process? And I started having a conflict about it. as I was doing it with the New Republic piece, I go to my niece who's 22 years old, and I go to her and I'm like, "what do young people wear right now?" I'm polling people to figure out how am I making this feel like young bodies? And she's like, we just wear street wear and stuff like that now. And I'm just looking through websites and looking at stuff. I'm like, God, they're so boring. Their colors are so boring. These kids have nothing for me. And so then I'm like, ah, shit, how do I work with that? So I mean, it turns like that in moments like that, where as a painter, you do want to find things.

And I think it's hard for people to understand this. Even in the case of the Jennings painting, you have to find things that you want to actually paint and light or color or shape or composition or characters or narrative. There's something that has to be the hook. And if there are no hooks or the hooks seem kind of weak, then it gets shitty. But there was this moment where I made this thing and it was like, this is not even the conversation that I had with these people. There was a lot of conversation with them about celebrity and public interaction and how that creates a sense in a condition to get young people to vote, which was kind of, I don't know, problematic for me, but that's their words, that's their thinking.

So for me, when I started thinking about it, that's why I pretty much just took the block that the Robeson House is on and made that, and they're on a corner. So then they become the start of the block. And I started thinking about a vessel at night, like a boat in the middle of the night in the ocean, and thinking about it being on a journey and what it's like to be on a ship at night. And it's very dark and there's only the moonlight and the stars that really guide you. And this idea of constellations as a way, as an agreed-upon form, and as a way for us to navigate space for us to understand our relationship in the world. And so then could that constellation be an America or at least the United States? And that is just an agreed-upon construct that we all live with inside of at this moment. But yes, as a construct, it can be deconstructed. So it does not mean that we all agree upon its formation of this constellation. So that's where it took me. And so that was an exciting proposition for me when I started thinking about it like that.

Daniel: Well, it's cool to hear about how you move through a process of solicitation and invitation and then weave it back into your work. I mean, for what it's worth, when I look at them, I think it's really effective as a series, because you do have these ideas that build on themselves. I think a constellation feels like it's in dialogue in an interesting way with a book called "The Plan" or with the kind of forward momentum of a crowd in the other painting.

Mark: Yeah, I was thinking about the movement with the crowd and compo-
sitionally, except for the boat, except for the housing thing, which possibly
has an east to west movement…for the most part, I was trying to get all
the bodies move west to east in kind of an anti manifest destiny gesture.

Daniel: Oh, interesting. So I guess using that reference in terms of the history
of painting, I want to pull back and talk a little bit more about the original
Jennings painting, just to get your take. You've also made this work that
part of your contribution to "Beyond Glass Cases," which is a poster-size
version of your ongoing "Town Crier" comic, and you analyze the Jennings
painting, and you also bring a critical assessment of that painting in through
the comic. And so I'm just wondering, one of the things you said is that this
original painting was kind of unusual in some respects. Maybe it wasn't that
unusual for the time, but it's unusual in retrospect in terms of this dialogue
between the artist and the recipients of the work at the Library Company.
Can you talk a little bit about what you see in that painting and how you
understand that dialogue between the Library Company and Jennings as
the artist? Something you said in your comic was that you thought that it
might have been a kind of version of virtue signaling for that time period

Mark: Yeah, I think it, it's a complicated painting because it's…an artifact
that sums up so many of the fricking weird things about our country where
statements are made and actions are not taken, where investments are placed
but not secured. It was tough to write that poster because there's so much
more—so trying to be economical, and it's not economical at all. It's a
pretty ranty thing I wrote.

But it was just simply like we, especially right now, in this moment, are
living in a time where there's severe crazy crap happening and people are
not doing anything about that. And the energy, especially at that moment
around the time when I was making this, there had been this moment in
the last six years or so, which goes back, I think, further than that. I think
if you're in the arts, it's been going on for more than a decade. But I think
more for the general public, this idea of how do we become the best versions
of ourselves and what does that mean? And do we have the ability with this
knowledge, with this technology, with this internet, with all this kind of
stuff, to learn so much about each other and to reconcile all that information
and to try to make a world where all of these bodies are represented. That's
what some people have tried to attach themselves to.

But I think that the translation between Jennings' original approach of
saying, do you want something that's of Minerva, or do you want something

of these very particular Greek goddesses? But then the [Library Company was] like, no, we want liberty and we want, and as they described these Negroes in the back frolicking, I forget the proper language of the piece, what they said in the statement, so please don't quote me on that, but that it was almost like a minor part to the actual library itself, which was to have the books and have these very particular books and have their catalog reside on top of that, sitting down next to her and these other things kind of laying on the ground. The interaction between her and these actual freed people is not a major part of the conversation for him, for the Library Company. [Jennings] chooses to bring them into the room. He chooses to have her interact with them in some way. He chose to create the dialogue between Liberty and the family. And I think there's so many things that are happening technically with just rendering people that creates a lot of conflict in this painting.

I mean, I sat with this painting so many times and not until a later time that I sat down, well after I made my own paintings, I'm like, "is the guy in red, the son? And is the guy in the vest, the father? Is there a relationship there between the father or son and the baby and the mother and you listen to?

And that was the thing about having everyone come in and kind of look at it, is that you got to hear everyone's interpretations of what this work is and what it means to them. I think we [got] the most generic versions of how someone could read a painting, of course. And I think that's also because we have to think about how we see narratives play out in artwork and how we see narratives play out in film and television and everything else. So there's things and concepts and visual things and practices that are here in this painting that really reflect what 1790 is. Not 2025. People look at a painting and they see time in such a bizarre way. They look at a painting of Jesus and they think that's what Jesus looked like. They look at a painting of anything and they think that's what it is, and that is who we are as humans. It's a problem.

So this image, even though it's fantasy, the relationships between who these characters are, what they're doing, because you could look at those four individuals and we know who they are, know they're slaves. We know that they've been freed. Are they freed? Are they on their way to being freed? There's all this conversation that people bring to it; people don't know what that is today here in this country. So they don't even go for that. No one even looked at that and possibly saw it as a sign of surrender. No one even thought about it in any of these terms. And I wonder about the frame of thinking in the speed of the read in the contemporary sense, to not even think about breaking down these elements. And it is like, who do I fault for that? Because it's not Black bodies who have this issue. It's all of our bodies who have these issues of our read of understanding the lack of complexity and the lack of nuance in the conversation.

I felt, if anything, anytime I would bring some kind of condition of nuance to Jennings, the painting, [or] The Library Company—that was almost seen as if I was acquiescing to something. And I am like, whoa, no, I'm not. I'm just saying as a maker, there are so many crazy factors that come into play. And I think in some ways, talking, in briefly talking about Benjamin Franklin in that "Town Crier" poster piece, I was trying to say he possibly was a slave owner. And then he goes from that period of his life, and as we look at Benjamin Franklin's life and how he changes in so many multiple ways from being a loyalist to being a part of the revolution, he also ends up becoming an abolitionist. That is his life, that is his complexity, that he did not get hatched in one way. He's some kind of NPC (non-player character) and then just operates on that same level his entire life. No one does and no one should. And hopefully, thank God, if that's possible, that means we least have an opportunity to grow and change.

Daniel: Well, it seems potentially a really, not that you would repeat this project again, but it seems like potentially a really generative tactic to use to have conversations with people about history paintings and then use them as sort of some fodder for your work, because there's a lot there.

Mark: Yeah, I mean, there's a possibility of doing it. Again, I would love to maybe try to do it for 2026, but that means I have to start today. It takes forever to do something like this. But I think that we are, I can't even begin at this point to think about what is actually missing and what needs to be addressed as far as our understanding of our current state of reality.

But I realized that I'm kind of a political junkie. I'm someone who actually likes to read a lot of different things about a lot of different positions in our country, and not everyone's like that. And I was thinking about this, this morning that people are like, well, I don't have time for that. And I was like, well, I pay my bills. I have a job. I actually have a job, and then I have another job because I want to try to be an artist as well. I have a wife, I have a home, I have a mortgage, I have to pay for a car. I have to keep electricity on. So I am not just sitting here just looking at this screen doing this.

But I do think that some people are called to be engaged with this thing and others are not. And I would think that in the moment that has happened in the last five, six years, that it would've raised the level of engagement and would've raised the level of stakes and understanding through all the conversation and the discourse that occurred. But it did not stick. And I'm kind of curious about that now. I'm kind of curious about why didn't it stick? What does it mean to have your rights removed from you in real time, and what does it mean that there are protests happening right now in this country all over this country and it's not being televised? I think about what that means at a place of high-density social media, and yet we're not collectively seeing the opposition to this reality.

What [is the] role of a painting as an article or an object of memory mean inside of that space? I think that the collective reinterpretation of what this painting is, is I'm happy that the language and the letters that were written about this work were not lost to history. They're very important. I think that the object can become a tool to learn through, but I find that the level of which young people and many people want to expedite its reasoning and its understanding of what this work is, before doing any of the actual labor of understanding how it was built and why it was built—really speaks to our time. And not in great ways.

Perhaps a little sidebar, I sit on a board member of this one institution where we had a person who was a pro-Palestinian artist who was vehemently "river to the sea." Many things that could possibly really be seen as antisemitic to a lot of the Jewish people also on this board to a T. Every person on the board who is Jewish fought for this person's rights as an American to say what they wanted to say and still exhibited the work. Now we have an artist who is of Israeli descent who makes pretty weird paintings about just open landscapes. And the whole younger side of the community that we work with all have threatened to quit. [This artist] they're anti Netanyahu, also anti-war, but yet the students, these young people are like, "they're Israeli. We don't want anything to do with them."

And I, being the non-Jewish body in the space, and I guess being a Black somewhat progressive person, my job is then to go in and say, these individuals who actually feel completely threatened by this situation allowed for somebody and fought for someone legally for them (because we had a bunch of lawyer shit that had to go on for this person to be here)—and you do not respect that at all. And you think that this action that you're going to take is somehow your beliefs, this is your position. And I am like, that is so thin and it lacks complexity,

And this is the problem right now, in this moment. We are living in a time where you need real, real problem-solving. The kind of things you learn from being an artist, the kind of things you learn in art school, the kind of things that you learn in music and theater and all these other things, the arts, the things that have been so heavily defunded in this country is that you learn how to think. There's many things that we teach in schools that do not teach thinking, critical thinking. I had a kid [in my class] who was doing advertising, and he just completely couldn't understand why we would even go in and critique an artwork and try to break it down. He was just like, "it's just a thing. It's just a thing. You're just handing in the thing, and that's the thing." And I was just like, "holy shit." I know it's a complete sidebar, but....

Daniel: But it's definitely relevant in terms of thinking about the value of maintaining these objects.

Mark: Yes. They must be maintained. They must be maintained. It's like then if you are not going to maintain the art objects, if you're not going to maintain the books, if you're not going to maintain Mark Twain, if you're not going to maintain Martin Luther King, if you're not going to maintain any of these things that have happened inside of this country that are relevant to the conformation of who we are and where we're at today, and you're just willing to toss it all out because it's complicated, then that means that you were not prepared to actually have a country because it is complicated.

Daniel: I think this is a good moment to ask my final question, which pulls back a little bit from your project and is about "Beyond Glass Cases" more generally as an initiative of the Library Company. My understanding of the project is that it had a few goals. One was to deal with controversial objects in their collection. One was to think about exhibition strategies more generally, and then the other one is about the potential role of artists within this organization interpreting their collection and making other kinds of interventions and contributions. So I'm just wanting to hear your take about the overall project goals, how you saw them interacting. Were there other kind of goals you brought into the process that changed or altered that? Just your sense of the overall project?

Mark: I think I kind of spoke to my goals with what I knew I needed to understand about the current state of politics. I think for them, I think the question is always going to be a complicated one because I think that in any institution, your goal[s], especially in a place like the Library Company, is to some degree…is to serve a community. The complication with that type of service is that you're servicing a community, meaning that there are many, many, many stakeholders and many, many people who have their own point of view.

I commend them for this openness. I commend them for their patience in this process. It is not easy to say, I'm going to commit money, time, and headspace for over a year to do something like this, and to not know exactly what the form is going to take in the end, that's insanely difficult, especially at this time. So I think that I would say one of the major strengths of their whole project is that I think that they're learning as they're doing it. I don't think that from my interactions with the Library Company that there was any real static pushback at all towards anything that I would want to do. It was more so that the conversation that I would hear from people outside of the space would describe the space as a space of pushback, which is strange that there was already, and I think that's something to be said of Philadelphia as a whole, is that there's a clear mistrust of institutions in the city. And I think sometimes it's earned and sometimes it is not.

Daniel: Yeah. But in terms of when you said you encountered that, is that something that seemed like it was grounded in actual experiences or was it more of a perception of this is conservative kind of history institution?

Mark: Yeah, it was just mostly perception. I would ask for detail, I would ask. I felt like it got to such a strange point for me with people where I would ask them, well, what happened? What do you know? What is a thing? And in that they would give me nothing. It was really strange.

Usually for me as an artist, I think about intent and I think about how many, I usually try to have max three intentions. In the case for what you just described in relationship to the Library Company, you stated that they had three goals. I'd be curious for them to really sit down and look at these three goals and see if they met them and not to beat themselves up over whether or not they didn't meet all three. Hell, if you meet one of the three goals, that's pretty damn hard. And I think that's how I look at it. That's how I look at working with them. I think that they did meet a lot of their goals, those three goals. I think they did do it. I just think, what is the next step?

Daniel: Right? How does that affect their ongoing work?

Mark: Yeah. How does that affect their ongoing work? How does that affect their next stage of this thing? Are there other complexities and other conversations that are possible there? And how do they highlight that it's an ongoing thing? And if anything, I would say they possibly need clarity over the stewardship of that role, meaning you want to create a true system of continuity in these endeavors. Because often what occurs is that one group of people come in and they take this thing on, and then it's not properly addressed, archived, stored, or even used as an entry point for individuals who are coming into this conversation. So for anyone who comes into this next stage of this, or if they decide to continue it, they really should probably have an onboarding where this work and the work of previous people are addressed.

Daniel: Well, it seems particularly relevant as I think at the closing reception that we were both at last week, there was an acknowledgment that there had been a lot of staff turnover. And so that obviously creates different levels of investment. So yeah, those transitions have big implications, not only for the project as it's unfolding, but obviously also its kind of legacy as well.

Mark: Well, it is a complicated thing. This kind of language isn't really what I wanted to use, but I think, I wonder how many people jumped ship but then didn't go back to look at what occurred. You know what I mean? Like if someone leaves a space in the middle of a project, how often do they ever go back to see how the project turned out? And it could have been that the project turns out great. And then it's like, well, what do you do with that? How do you reconcile that? I think the narrative that a lot of people have towards the possibility of acknowledging what's really occurring.

And I saw that with that Jennings painting again and again. That I was trying to describe the supplicant slave to people and the wedgewood pottery, and even what the whole use of that object was used for to raise money for to do X, Y, Z thing. And that this figure with this man who's bowing with his hand on his head is not the supplicant slave. He's not there with chains that are up in the air and asking to be freed. He's in the post-state of that. He is acknowledging that this thing has occurred. And the dynamic of whether or not whiteness as a body had the power condition to offer freedom to Blacks is something that I think for some people is frustrating, and they're unable to come to terms with it that yeah, you were in an object position. You did not have the ability to free yourself. It took white bodies to do that work to actually allow for that to occur. How do you reconcile that with your ideas that white people are evil? How do you reconcile that with other issues you may have, or you're in the Kanye West camp where you think all Blacks should have just freed themselves because they just should have; there's a historical understanding of reality and we're not teaching it, so where are we?

And so as an artist making this work,…[what] I had to think about was [if it was] my duty to be an historian, is [it also] my duty to be the artist who's making the work? Where do I sit? As an artist working on this thing, you start to go through this process of like, is it my job to be a historian? But then I'm like, I don't even know where to start with some people. And the clarity of having the history teachers there was that I felt like we're all on the same page and that they were able to be, there were bodies that can hold this space of complexity, of density, and then while trying to operate in the reality of our day today, that is not a space I think that many people can hold. And also just because it's difficult does [not] mean that it's difficult for me to hold that.

But that is why there's a Library Company. That is why there are librarians. That is why there are researchers. That is why that these people exist in the world. Just because it's difficult and it's hard does not mean that we don't have the resources placed inside of our society for individuals like this. And for spaces like this, it is a necessity that we have it. And I think that the frustrations and the making and the creation and the formation and the time period and the length of which to do all of this was extremely necessary for results to occur. And I commend everyone at the Library Company past and present and my time working there because all of them were committed to doing this work and to making this show happen fully.

Daniel: Well, my engagement is definitely to critically assess and reflect on its implications for not only the Library Company, but also for the field. Which as you kind of allude to with the 2026 stuff is in a total moment of crisis in terms of the ways in which the critical aspirations of some organizations to reassess the history of this country are being thwarted and complicated by some of the changes that are happening in terms of federal policy.

Mark: It's a complicated, weird moving target that we're on. It is complicated, and it isn't complicated. It's not that complicated because if your job is to hold history, and to report history, then that's just your job that if there's someone who's trying to stop you from doing that work, then that means that they have a problem. And the only complication is the stress and the idea of trying to uphold your beliefs. That's it. And that's not that big of a deal if you think about it in the long term.

Project Obtuse By Zachariah Julian and Paul Wolff Mitchell

"Crania Americana and the Archive of Scientific Racism"
August 19, 2024–October 30, 2024

"Project Obtuse"
September 17, 2024

In "Project Obtuse," Jicarilla Apache artist Zachariah Julian used color, sound, and movement to confront a dark chapter in the history of indigenous peoples in America. Julian examined the work of Samuel George Morton, whose papers reside, in part, at the Library Company. Morton is known today as among the most influential architects of scientific racism in the United States, both for his publications—most notably "Crania Americana" (1839)—and for his collection of nearly one thousand human skulls from across the world, amassed and measured during his lifetime to supply the "data" for these works. Scholar and former Library Company Fellow Paul Wolff Mitchell conducted a thorough study of the Morton Papers across several repositories. For "Project Obtuse", Mitchell worked with Julian to explore how Morton's thinking developed and how his theories still impact us today. Through composition and performance, Julian shifted our gaze away from the chapter written by Morton and his colleagues and toward a thriving present and future that Indigenous Americans write for themselves.

"Project Obtuse" included an exhibition, "Crania Americana and the Archive of Scientific Racism," curated by Paul Wolff Mitchell. The evening after the exhibition opened, Julian's live performance "Project Obtuse" debuted at the Asian Arts Initiative, and was immediately followed by a panel discussion with Julian and Mitchell, led by Library Company Curator of Printed Books Rachel D'Agostino.

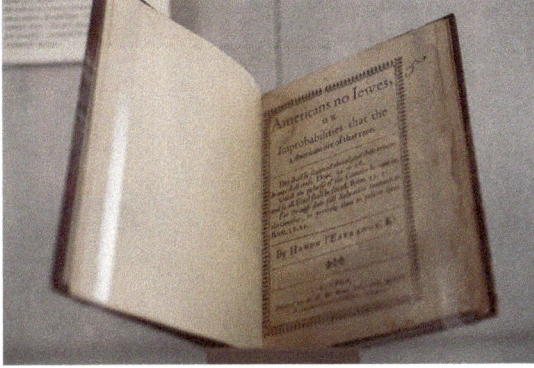

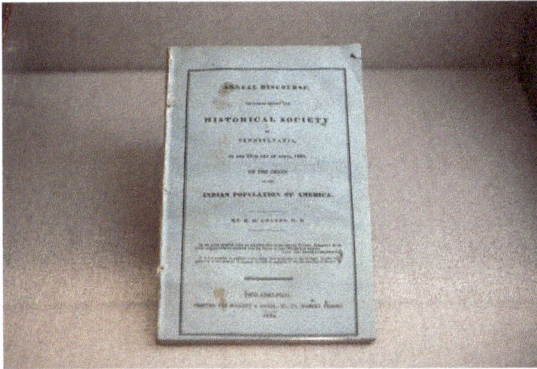

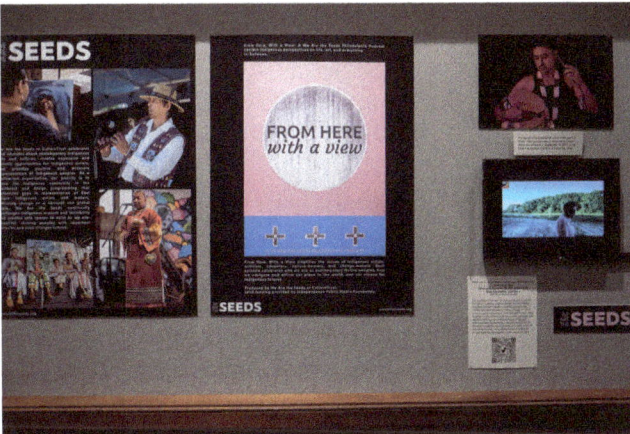

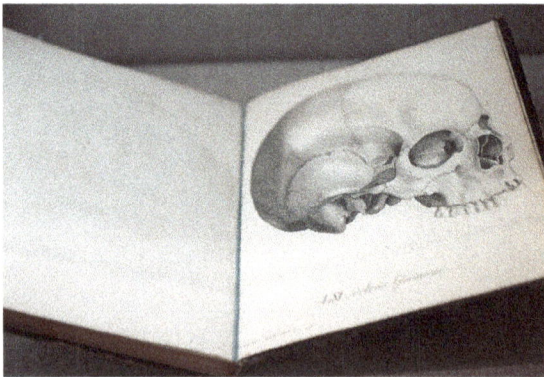

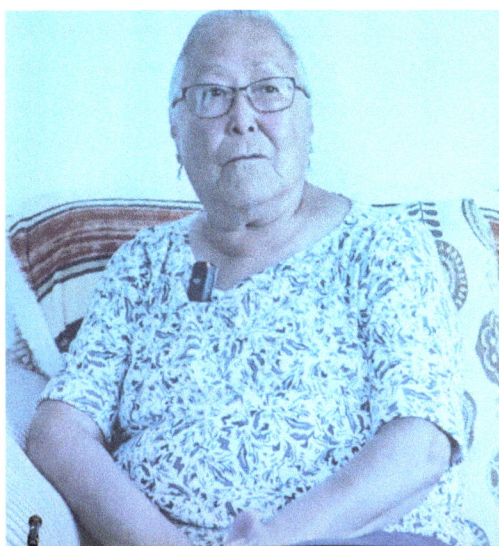

Interview: Zachariah Julian

This interview was conducted by Daniel Tucker on April 17, 2025.

Daniel: I wanted to talk a little bit about pre-history. I realize that's very broad, but can you talk a little bit about the kind of projects that you were working on before, "Beyond Glass Cases?" What did your practice look like? Maybe you could share a little bit about your history with We Are the Seeds, and then we'll talk about your individual practice too.

Zachariah: Prior to "Beyond Glass Cases," I was working on honing my composition style, practice, and production. I was recording a lot of music at a studio in Albuquerque, and I was learning a lot from the producer that worked there. I had released a demo of my music a few years earlier and I could hear all of my weaknesses, so I really buckled down and started taking my practice seriously. I threw the Blues scale into my piano practice and that opened the door to Jazz. I practiced piano every day. I used to put on these long YouTube videos of trains traversing the land of some European country and I would just practice while enjoying the scenery. As for performing, I would get shows at a lot of Native events, like Gathering of Nations, cultural centers, and at art events. Then one day, I got hired to perform in Santa Fe, New Mexico, and that's where I met Tailinh Agoyo, the founder of We Are the Seeds. We became good friends. We started talking and emailing. And then it was like six months, she asked if I'd like to perform at the Pequot Museum in Connecticut. I ended up composing a musical in three months and premiered it there. And so, I kept working with Seeds. Then, a couple of years later, We Are the Seeds collaborated with the Philadelphia Orchestra for their YouTube project: "Our City, your Orchestra"—that episode got nominated for an Emmy. A lot of people don't know that.

Daniel: Oh, wow. I didn't know that.

Zachariah: I can actually say I'm an Emmy-nominated artist. Wild! It was a group effort, and we all worked very hard on that episode. It came out beautifully. After I worked with the Philadelphia Orchestra, more projects started popping up. Soon after, I got the email about "Beyond Glass Cases".

Daniel: Great. And so I mean, before we go there, I'm wondering, were you doing, what kind of compositions were you working on prior to the Seeds? Were you working in a really collaborative fashion? Was it mainly solo? What did it sort of look like?

Zachariah: I grew up singing in a metal band on the rez, and at the same time I was also learning piano. I was obsessed with Beethoven sonatas, so I was kinda between words. I loved metal music but I also enjoyed the romantic era of classical music. I left the band when I started going to college, and I mainly focused on solo work. I really fell in love with the singer/songwriter path, as a musician. It allowed me to compose in any style that I wanted. I spent many years working on my artistic voice and musical style. Eventually, I met with a music producer, and I started collaborating with other musicians again.

Right before "Beyond Glass Cases," I got a residency at a dance studio called Keshet, in Albuquerque. It prepared me a lot for "Beyond Glass Cases." I was working with a choreographer. I had access to a big stage that had a projector and a big screen. Keshet had everything. And as an artist, seeing my music put to motion was a dream come true. I grew up wanting to compose music for movies and video games, and out of left field, I was working with dancers. It was a wonderful experience.

Daniel: And are those kind of commissions, or are they just your own independent music practice?

Zachariah: It's a mix of both.

Daniel: I'm wondering if you could talk a little bit about how We Are the Seeds was approached about "Beyond Glass Cases," what those early conversations were before there was a project in mind?

Zachariah: I got an email from Tailinh, and she was like, "Hey. Don't be mad at me, but there are some people looking for an Indigenous artist, and I threw your name into the pool and now they want to talk to you."

So I met with them; it was Paul Wolff Mitchell and Rachel D'Agostino. They shared what the project was and told me to think it over. I remember Tailinh and I spoke immediately after the meeting, [but] we were a little hesitant. This was new territory for Seeds. Our focus has always been on the joy of Indigeneity and uplifting Native creatives, "Beyond Glass Cases" was a new path for us, but we knew we could do it. I'm glad we did. About a week later I got word from Tailinh that they had picked me for the project.

Daniel: And so Paul Wolff Mitchel was there from the start, but then there were also people from the Library Company, presumably. And so was it already conceptualized that this would be in dialogue with Paul's research that they were already doing?

Zachariah: Yes. It was important that I tell this dark part of U.S. history from the Indigenous perspective, that these four cases on exhibit at the

Library Company had an Indigenous response. It was also important for us to not show any of the skulls that Morton used. We wanted to respect our ancestors.

Daniel: And you talked on the podcast about the research being really difficult, that it made you angry, and that it was ultimately difficult to perform. I have some questions later about the performance, but I was wondering: when you were making visits to the Library Company, what were you looking at in the archives? Just to give us a sense of materially, what were you looking at and [have] you done that kind of archival work before? Or was this, I mean, it sounds like you're saying this wasn't really material that you had looked at before.

Zachariah: I never worked on something like this before. I had access to Samuel Morton's papers, his diary, his writings, and letters from people wanting to donate to his collection. Every visit I made to the Library Company, Rachel would have some books pulled aside for me that would inspire me. I remember asking her if she could dig up books about the Southwest and anything they had about my people—the Apaches. She brought me U.S. cavalry reports, newspapers, journals from settlers living in the Southwest; there wasn't much info, but the information I got was very helpful. It helped me understand the ideology of the United States Government and Native nations that had been occupied. There is such a helpless feeling reading the propaganda used against your own people. It really opened my eyes to how the government works. Paul sent me books when the project first started. Paul and Rachel were very helpful and always available when I had questions or needed to vent. I was definitely overwhelmed when I first started, but they helped me a lot.

Daniel: I wasn't aware that you were looking at this other material outside of the Morton material, so it sounds like these calvary reports and scouting reports were things that were actually held in the Library Company's collection.

Zachariah: I read a lot. I remember on one of my visits, Rachel had brought out a bunch of old Cherokee newspapers. I was skimming through them and I came upon an ad. I took a picture of it, because it just blew my mind. There were ads in a Native paper looking for scouts to help hunt down the Apaches. The cavalry reports were pretty brutal. Lots of death. But yeah, the propaganda was heartbreaking. One of the books Paul sent me was a book called "The Skull Collectors" by Ann Fabian. It focused on some influential people that were pushing pseudoscience, and how their influence was spreading in government institutions.

Daniel: Like Morton, right?

Zachariah: Yeah. It focuses on five scientists, and Morton is kind of in the middle, but there's two scientists before him that inspires his research, and that's what this book goes through. If anyone wants a brief overview of how someone like Morton rose to power, I recommend it.

Daniel: Tell me about what manifested in the cases themselves?

Zachariah: I remember talking to Paul and asking him for help. This was like June or July of 2024 and I was still in the middle of composing. I didn't have a beginning yet. I relied on him to pick the books which were very helpful. Seeing a linear story appear out of what I had already composed and created, was a good feeling. Watching it all come together. The first three cases would house books from the collection at the Library Company. The first case was about first contact, the second was about the United States government conquering and destroying Native land and culture, and the third held Morton's papers. The fourth and final case would be, what we called, the "Seeds" case. The Seeds case was dedicated to Native joy, resilience, and a reminder that we are still here. The United States government failed.

Daniel: And did that incorporate some of the other We Are the Seeds projects and ephemera? Or what was contained there?

Zachariah: It had some of our projects. Tons of pictures and information about us. There was also a tablet in the case that was playing highlights from our podcast "From Here, with a View," where we interviewed a lot of well-known, famous indigenous artists, musicians, scientists, farmers, just the whole spectrum of indigeneity. The case was a symbol of resilience, a collective voice, fighting back against the erasure that exists so heavily across this country.

Daniel: I want to talk a little bit about the performance then. So "Project Obtuse" ended up being songs and video, and formally, it included many different elements. It was certainly a transmedia production including the painting that you were doing on and near the screen on the plexiglass, there was film grain, and then there were these interviews including about your mom's boarding school experience. I just wrote down a couple of lines that stood out to me from your lyrics, which is obviously, it's just like a tiny excerpt of what you were saying, but you said things like, "This is what they do, they make science out of you. We existed, we resisted. They took us piece by piece, they changed the name, what we mean. My heart is on fire."

I guess I'm just wondering, with all that you brought together there, I want to understand a little bit more about your process. Can you talk about the decisions that you made as an artist about what to include, how to sequence it, and how imagery was paired with music in that sense?

Zachariah: The way I work is I always think of the biggest idea. When I first got this project, I was like, this would make such an interesting opera, but I don't have the money or the stage for an opera, so what's the next level down? I just kept chiseling the idea down till all I had were the core elements: my mother's story, Morton's Papers, the United States government, and present-day Natives. I could have composed a response that was just music, but that felt a little empty to me. "Beyond Glass Cases" was about sight. It was about looking back at our shared history. I didn't want people to come to my performance just to listen. Morton stripped away the identity of our ancestors. I wanted to give some identity back.

Just before this project, I had a residency at a dance studio, which allowed me to try mixed media for the first time. They had this beautiful theater where you can project stuff, and I've always wanted to do that. I grew up really listening to Nine Inch Nails, really liking David Lynch and this kind of mix of media for the sake of texture. You were talking about grain, texture was important to me. You see this grainy imagery, and that was to symbolize that this is the past. And when I get to my mom, that grain goes away. And then after my mom's story, it's gone. The grainy texture never returns. When I edited the video that accompanied my performance, tone was the most important to me.

I never know what to say when someone asks about my artistic process. Because honestly, I have no idea how a lot of what I create comes to be. That's the truth. And so when I listen or watch a piece that I've composed, I go, "wow, look at that. I put that there perfectly." It's this artistic side that comes out of you when you just trust yourself and your process.

Daniel: This is sort of a two-part question, I'm wondering about how you think the work would live outside of the framework of "Beyond Glass Cases." If that was something that you were thinking about while you were making it, or if you were sort of like, no, this is site specific—this is for this project "Beyond Glass Cases" for The Library Company, for this research around scientific racism. I know you made a decision not to include that imagery from the collection, but I'm also wondering how you think about the way that the performance was contextualized or determined by the Library Company kind of holdings.

Zachariah: I do see this continuing. I do want to perform it again and again. I left it open-ended because I realized there's no way I can end this. I kind of struggled with the ending there, but then I realized there is no ending. This story is continuing. And I like that because then I can start putting in new pieces. I can start venturing into new topics. I would love to have a section about the Trail of Tears. Let's bring in people to have these discussions. Let's collaborate with the elders and the people who are well versed in this. I think it's something that can really branch out and become whatever it needs to be in order to fit where it's being performed and tell those stories—locally.

Daniel: Do you have any recollections of what the conversation after the performance was like?

Zachariah: Honestly, it's kind of a blur. Yeah.

Daniel: I'm sure it's hard to do right after you perform this epic piece too.

Zachariah: Yeah. I remember finishing the piece and I started crying. I didn't want people to see, so I went into the green room, and I was trying really hard not to punch a hole in the wall. My wife came back and just held me, and soon after, Max, our photographer for Seeds and a dear friend of mine, came into the back to check on me. We're a close-knit family. I eventually went back out onto the stage so we could start the Q&A portion of the performance. I was more nervous about the Q&A section than the performance. I was ready for questions about the piece, but, out of all the questions, only one person asked me about the music and my process, but Paul and Rachel were there to really help stabilize me and talk about the project.

Daniel: You mentioned that a lot of the questions weren't really about the piece.

Zachariah: So yeah, there was a guy walking around with a wireless mic and people would raise their hands and ask their questions.

Daniel: Were they asking you for historical context or were they asking you personal questions? Do you have a sense of where that was coming from?

Zachariah: It was never the things that inspired certain sections or my artistic process. It was more like, God, I wish I could remember, but it was just more about Morton and the research. Which I understand, but I wanted to talk about the music.

Daniel: Yeah. Do you think that that is a reflection of the fact that the audience coming from The Library Company?

Zachariah: There were some people from the Library Company, not much. They had their crew there helping set up and stuff. Most of the people that were there, I'm guessing, found out through We Are the Seeds, social media, and some of the advertising that the Library Company was doing. They didn't look familiar.

Daniel: I think that in some ways I'm more interested in both what was your experience of performing it, but then also what kind of feedback and responses you got? And it sounds like you said it was really difficult for you to do. That's a lot to put yourself through. Is that a place that you want to go, or do you prefer to make work kind of in a different mode?

Zachariah: The performance was well received. I remember people lining up after the Q&A to talk to me. I heard a lot of positive feedback. People were thanking me for helping them feel and understand the pain of my ancestors and modern-day Natives. I remember going out and having a nice dinner with my friends afterwards. It was a very surreal moment. It was over but it still hadn't hit me yet.

I tend to drown myself in the piece I'm creating. I have really bad depression, but I've learned how to use it for my artistic advantage. I've learned how to pick myself back up after completing a piece. "Project Obtuse" was a nine-month project for me, so I spent a lot of time in these dark mental spaces. It was just this constant balance of taking care of myself, my mental health, trying to make sure my body doesn't completely turn on me, I started doing Tai Chi again, which really, really helped. But that's the way I work. I put 100% of myself into these pieces emotionally. This is what art is, this is the way it should be. I mean, I don't mean to stand on a soapbox and say those things.

Daniel: I may return to that, but I am thinking about the project more generally. So this publication is going to be about the overall "Beyond Glass Cases" project. And when I talk to the Library Company staff, there's often a couple of different goals that they identified for the project. One is this focus on controversial objects. Some of it is about rethinking how they make exhibitions, and then some of it is about engaging artists and artists as interpreters of their collection. And so I guess stepping back from the specifics of your piece a little bit, I'm wondering how you experienced that overall project of the "Beyond Glass Cases" initiative. In what ways did you see examples of them stretching as an organization to either fit your project or explore these goals that they had?

Zachariah: I don't think that it was ever like that. It was very natural. There was never any really butting of heads or anything like that. We would have monthly meetings. I would have monthly meetings with Paul and Rachel, and we'd have conversations, and I ended up talking to somebody from the Pew as well. But it was just discussing the cases and the performance in the piece and just kind of checking in on how I'm doing and where it's at. Because the way I work is I write two pieces. So I was actually writing two pieces at once, and I was kind of putting all my energy into one piece, and I realized this isn't going to work. And having these conversations with Paul and Rachel going, okay, I need to readjust. And that's just the natural way of work. I realize I work best when I meet people halfway.

Daniel: Well, and to be clear, I didn't mean to suggest that it was a tension or anything, more just that they committed themselves as an organization to explore these different ways of working that maybe weren't necessarily typical for them. And so I'm just trying to get a sense of…for participants where it's like you don't have an ongoing role at the Library Company, obviously. Right. So your investment is your artwork. As an artist, I'm imagining your investment is more in your practice and not in the Library Company changing how they make exhibitions. But I was just trying to get a sense of how did different participants in the project perceive the kind of goals of "Beyond Glass Cases?"

Zachariah: I realized while working on this project that the Library Company had never done anything like this before. They were in the same boat as me, which made me feel better about what I was doing. What do we do with this sensitive material? How do we talk about his sensitive material? It was a learning experience, I think, for both of us. Rachel said something to me that gave me hope. It was along the lines of, "this is the way it should be done. This is the way we have these conversations and what "Beyond Glasses Cases" is all about." It's two sides coming together to have a conversation about a dark part of this country's history. We both learn from one another, and I think that is the best way to do it.

Daniel: That's great. I appreciate that. I mean, in some ways it makes me wonder, how does an organization build that into their process moving forward? And to some extent, that's a question as much for the Library Company as it is [for] We Are the Seeds. Do you have a sense of how the Seeds would approach this kind of opportunity again in the future, or how you would as an individual?

Zachariah: We learned a lot as an organization, and we are definitely ready to take on more projects like "Beyond Glass Cases." "Project Obtuse" will live on, [and] I'm excited to see what it will grow into. I'm ready. This project taught me a lot about myself and how I work. I grew a lot over the nine-month project, even though it felt like years.

Interview: Paul Wolff Mitchell

This interview was conducted by Daniel Tucker on May 1, 2025.

Daniel: I was wondering if you could share a little bit about the prehistory of this work for you. I know that you also had a prehistory with the Library Company in addition to this, so we can talk about that, but I'm also wondering more generally about your engagement with critical museology and your research more broadly.

Paul: Sure. Yeah. My PhD is in anthropology. Initially, probably as a response to a conservative, religious upbringing, I was particularly interested in human evolution. So I studied biological anthropology and focused on the study of human skeletal remains, whether those were ancient and fossil, or comparatively more recent. But by the time that I was getting into my dissertation research, working in the Penn Museum, it became very clear to me that there was something very big I had missed in my training, working as a scientist with human remains.

I had worked with a collection of human remains as a research assistant in the museum, including the curation of a collection of human skulls. They were amassed in the nineteenth century by a physician and naturalist, Samuel George Morton, and those skulls would be used for example, by other researchers as comparative samples, for example, for biomedical studies or as they would be measured as comparative samples for comparisons within archeological or paleoanthropological studies. And, initially, I viewed them that way, too, primarily as objects. But, there were a number of uncomfortable incidents over time that compounded, that made me realize that there was something I had missed: the history of these remains and a critical look at what brought them into the museum. I remember in particular that I was tasked to teach in a room as a graduate student where the skulls were on display, around 2017 or so. And these skulls amassed by Morton often had labels pasted on their foreheads.

And I remember a student who I later came to learn, both of his parents were from Nigeria. He asked me why there were these skulls in cabinets on the wall with labels on their foreheads, labels stating that they were from Black people from Africa. And I explained that Morton had collected and measured these skulls in the context of nineteenth-century anthropology, that these were from people who were enslaved and died in Cuba in the 1830s. The museum didn't warn or inform students, or instructors, about any of this before assigning courses in this room filled with skulls on cabinets on the wall. And, I could see in this student's face that the more that I explained the details, the more that the explanation was uncomfortable for this student, literally faced with the skulls in front of him. And I realized that putting these skulls on display without context, continuing to view them as mere scientific objects, we were not approaching this history carefully. And indeed the further I went into the history behind these remains, the more troublesome this became for me. And those sorts of experiences, that's one of a few, ultimately led me to think much more seriously about what it was that I was doing there with that collection of skulls. And ultimately, I focused my research on the history of not just the Morton collection, but human cranial collections in the nineteenth and late eighteenth century generally.

My dissertation ended up focusing on really the practice of collecting human skulls for racial science in the period from about 1750 until about 1850. And I put Morton's collection in context with the European collections that were the prompt and the inspiration for what Morton was doing, but putting all of this from this broader sort of scientific racism within the context of the global imperial and colonial networks in which it arose and by which it was possible. So I knew more than a little bit about Morton by the time that the "Beyond Glass Cases" project arose. I actually was a fellow at the Library Company previously, supported by the Library Company and the Consortium for History of Science, Technology and Medicine, as a big part of my research was looking at the Morton Papers, and especially the correspondence archive that is spread between the Library Company and the American Philosophical Society.

And a lot of those letters between about the 1830s and the 1850s detail how skulls came into Morton's collection. And a lot of my work was focused on that, both my academic work and some public-facing work, which generated some critical conversations at that museum and also was a part of changing practices at the museum where the skulls were taken off display, and ultimately there was a public commitment on the part of the museum to work toward returning or repatriating those remains to descendant communities whenever possible. That was a big shift between when I started this research and by the time I finished my dissertation in 2022, which is just about when the "Beyond Glass Cases" project was really coming into form. But yeah, I carried that with me at the start of the project.

Daniel: Well, kind of building off of that, I'm wondering, you had been a research fellow at the Library Company and I'm wondering how that sort of ended up either differing or overlapping with what came to be the "Crania Americana" project and how you ultimately came to be involved in "Beyond Glass Cases."

Paul: I was a short-term fellow at the Library Company around 2020. I started in January 2020 doing research on Morton's papers. I was looking at the manuscript of Morton's book, "Crania Americana". I was looking at this manuscript, and I discovered a lot of it was composed of pieces of paper glued together, mostly with wax. This was common in the nineteenth century, paper was expensive and they wouldn't waste it. So Morton would paste pieces of paper together to construct this manuscript, on what I presume was scrap paper on the other side.

And actually, although this was all pasted and glued together quite tightly, there are little bits and pieces on hundreds of pages that were loose. And I looked underneath, I saw there was writing on the other side in Morton's hand. And I told this to the then Librarian, Jim Green, who has since retired, and he looked at it with a lot of interest. He asked Jennifer Rosner, the head conservator at the Library Company, if we could open this up, to see what was on the underside of all these pieces of paper? Could we undo the glue? And the answer was yes, with some effort. And I found this completely unknown dimension to Morton's archive, all these notes and fragments that hadn't seen the light of day since Morton pasted this book together, including a lot that changes a lot of what we understand about how Morton got started in collecting skulls and his first and most consequential book on race, "Crania Americana." I'm currently working on a book about this, so that's all that I'll say for now.

Anyway, Jim was really interested. I was really interested. And then we had all these wonderful plans to work with Jennifer and open up all the backsides of the pieces of paper. And then COVID hit, so then everything was completely delayed, and the conservation work went really slowly over the next couple of years.

Pretty soon it became clear that this material wouldn't be ready to study before I was hoping to finish my PhD, in spring 2022, as I had gotten a job at the University of Amsterdam. I continued to work on other materials in the Morton papers in the Library Company while finishing up my dissertation. While I was doing so, Emily Guthrie had taken over as the Librarian replacing Jim after he retired. She had heard about my work from Jim and let me know that she was applying for this project and invited me to be involved.

Emily said it was an absolute long shot with the Pew Center for Arts and Heritage, dealing with difficult or problematic heritage and critical new experimental ways of dealing with it within the Library Company. And something around "Crania Americana," and something around this work with Morton, would potentially be really interesting. Would I be interested? And I said, sure. I partly said, sure, because I was reasonably certain that her assurance that this was a long shot meant that I probably wasn't signing up for much, and I didn't hear anything for a while. And it was really, I think after I had defended my dissertation that ultimately, or just around then it was confirmed ultimately that the project was going through and we were going to have to start thinking of, well, yeah, what are we going to do here? But it really grew organically out of the work that I was doing, trying to put this book "Crania Americana" in context.

Daniel: Yeah. That's great. Well, so at some point in that process, after you found out that there was a green light to go ahead, you came to work in some form, and I want you to describe it with We Are the Seeds. So how did you and Zachariah Julian come to collaborate on the exhibit? Just talk a little bit about how that collaboration started.

Paul: I had signed up with "Beyond Glass Cases" in effect from the beginning, and I knew that that meant that we were committed to having not just a scholarly or academic component to the project, but also to an artistic inter-vention. And it was also important given the nature of the material, that we really wanted to include Indigenous voices in a way that was going to put this history and some in the context in a different framing than it had been placed in the Library Company and elsewhere until that point. So really, it was a bit of a task to think, well, okay, we have the grant now. How are we going to actually make this history come alive and put in center Indigenous voices in the way that this history is presented through this project?

So, I had a conversation with someone I went to graduate school with. Her name is Stephanie Mach. She did her PhD at Penn as well. She's now a curator at the Harvard Peabody Museum. Stephanie is Indigenous herself. She's Diné (Navajo). She had for a long time been a critic of the way that the Morton collection was on display at the [Penn] Museum. And yeah, I think it's fair to say, a critic of my initial work with the collection. And really someone who helped me in my research and thinking and shifting my thinking about these histories. So I had a good connection with her, and she knew a lot about the topic, and she said, well, I said, this is what we're doing. I think it's really important that Indigenous voices are central here. And she said, "Talk to We Are the Seeds." So that was a serendipitous connection, but it was based upon the relationship I'd had with Stephanie thinking about these issues through graduate school together. And Stephanie herself is quite involved with We Are the Seeds and has known [the director Tailinh Agoyo] for a while. And so that's how it all [happened].

Daniel: And ultimately then, let's talk a little bit about how you all kind of worked together once Zacharia was on board. How did you all collaborate on the different components of the project?

Paul: Well, it was fascinating because the project, of course, is centered in Philadelphia. I got a postdoc in the Netherlands, where I'm talking to you from right now, and Zach lives in New Mexico. So we didn't actually meet physically until the performance, and we were operating across a nine-hour time difference. So as you can imagine, this was a bit of a challenge. It was all digital, but he is three hours as it were, behind Philly as it were, six hours ahead. So this was an interesting logistical challenge, but from across the ocean and a continent we connected often with Rachel D'Agostino at the Library Company, talking about how we were going to make this work together. And usually relatively late in the evening for me, relatively early in the morning for Zach and somewhere in between for Rachel, we would over a number of months talk, also sometimes just one-on-one, with Zach about how to make these archives accessible to what Zach wanted to do for an artistic intervention.

And [by] that I part meant showing the landscape, as it were, of this archive in relation to this broader history. And a lot of it really became, it became very personal for Zach, and ultimately for me too. But I think most importantly for Zach, because he talked about how he didn't learn about so much of this history when he grew up, but the way which it sort of embedded in the experiences particularly of his parents and the discrimination that they faced and the challenges that they [encountered] as Indigenous people, as Jicarilla Apache people in New Mexico, he's living on the reservation now, and these are histories that are very close and embodied and are a part of his lived experience and that of his parents and his community. But there was nothing about the intersection of settler colonialism and science that they learned in school in the context of a detailed historical explanation, certainly not with the kind of archival detail of the history laid out in front of him in the archives of the Library Company.

So it was really emotional, I felt, for Zach. And also then for me as well, to sort of be trying to approach this from the somewhat removed stance of a researcher, a scholar, and then being in conversation with someone for whom this was so immediately and directly moving, I often felt despite the actual physical distance between us, and the frustrations of online digital meetings, it was quite moving and quite personal. But a lot of this was talking about this history, talking about the archives, also working with Rachel to make sure that when Zach was present in Philadelphia, that the relevant material was available for him. And then talking with him when I was working on the installation in the Library Company, the kind of archival display that was kind of my part of the project that we were in conversation with, how that archival display would, as I put it, give footnotes to the [performance] presentation that he would do. And the manifestation of those footnotes, as it were, was the display in the Library Company in the gallery next to the reading room. And the performance was the real text.

Daniel: You talk about this installation that happened at the Library Company, one of the things I was struck by was your decision to turn the busts backwards. And I guess, I mean, that's maybe one decision, right? That's one exhibition decision, but I'm wondering if you could reflect also on any other that or other decisions that you made in order to situate this work within the institution?

Paul: I'm just flipping through my phone to look, because I've got the text from Rachel. We texted after she sent me a picture after she turned them around, basically that was a completely last minute and spontaneous decision because the installation was up. I mean, I spent, I dunno how many months picking out the materials. I went to Philly, at least one time, actively to spend a lot of time looking through the materials, picking them out, the actual archival materials that would go into the cases. I spent a lot of time writing all of the texts that you saw within the exhibit, but then the actual installation and manifestation, I wasn't there until after it was all up. And I remember when I saw it, I thought, well, this is interesting that we have this really critical view on the white supremacist underpinnings and legacies of this archive, which is what this critical exhibition is about. And then on the very top, literally on the top of the cases, we have a row of, oh, about six busts of eighteenth- and nineteenth-century white guys sitting on top of the exhibit. We thought: can we make this a statement, too? At first, the question was can we just move them? And that didn't really seem feasible on short order, but I think either Rachel or I said, "Hey, can we just turn these around?" And that was doable. So there was, of course, no text in the exhibit talking about that, but it was among the small symbolic gestures that are insufficient, but I think necessary to prick a critical consciousness about the institution's history, exactly what this sort of exhibition should generate. I still don't know who those guys are, and it's a wonderful little research question to critically sketch out who these figures are and their relationship to the institution, and so on. But the details didn't really matter to me. I just thought they should be turned around, as if we're seeing the backsides of the histories as they have often been presented.

Daniel: Can you share about the origin of the name "Project Obtuse" and its relationship to the history of chronology?

Paul: So this was Zach's idea, I have to say. Zach would often ask really open questions, out of a genuine sense of curiosity about not just the broad outlines of the history, but often honing in on specific details concerning the history of cranial race science. And I would go on and talk, and it wouldn't stop—I'm an academic. Then at certain points Zach would say, "Whoa, whoa. What did you say? Can you repeat that?" And one thing that happened was about the origins of this practice of collecting and measuring skulls and classifying them and comparing them, making hierarchies out of them on the basis of race. And that really traces to a Dutch anatomist, which is actually one of the reasons that I'm here now in the Netherlands.

Really about sixty years before Morton even started thinking about this, about eighty years before the publication of "Crania Americana," this eighteenth-century Dutch anthropologist, an anatomist named Petrus Camper, suggested a measurement of the skull that could be used to differentiate people from different continents, and it became a common metric for supposedly measuring race. This was a part of the Enlightenment drive to classify and measure everything. Actually, Morton measured skulls using the same measurement, as well as other ones. This measurement from Camper is called the facial angle, and it's basically a measurement of the projection of the jaw relative to the forehead. And so Camper arranged these skulls along this hierarchy stating that the smaller the facial angle, or basically the more that the jaw projects out in front of the face relative to the forehead, the more animal-like the skull is. This might be a dog, not a pug, but think like a greyhound, like with a long snout, or a bird, or for that matter, an ape.

They have jaws that project forward out relative to the forehead. But humans, relative to animals, all have relatively flat faces. Camper claims that you could use this measurement not just to differentiate animals and humans, but also human races. This was in the 1760s. And Camper said that the most beautiful and the most ideal human faces had the biggest facial angles. This was a part of a hierarchy of aesthetics for Camper, and that Europeans had the biggest facial angles. But what was curious is that when he drew this hierarchy, which of course in the same way that Morton's work has all been roundly refuted and shown to be full of biases, the same as applicable here. But one of the interesting things about this history is that when Camper made this, and it was very influential in the same way with deadly consequence, that Morton's work was influential.

But when Camper made this sort of comparison of skulls, the ideal form that he presented, the one with the biggest forehead, had a forehead that was anatomically impossible—that is to say it doesn't normally occur in people. And if it were to occur, it would look, well, extremely unusual. It would be an angle of 100 degrees; it would be a forehead that basically juts out in front of the face. I think I just said offhand, this head is what Camper suggested was the ideal of beauty, with an obtuse facial angle, it's more-or-less anatomically impossible. And then Zach said, "Whoa." Obviously, there's at least a double entendre about the obtuseness of the angle and the obtuseness of the measurer. That's sort of the genesis of this, yeah.

Daniel: And just I guess for clarifying purposes, do you look at it as kind of a dual name of the project, or is it like one is sort of nested within the other? How do you…?

Paul: Yeah, I think it's either or both, or I should put it this way: "Crania Americana and the Archive of Scientific Racism" is the archival installation under the broader "Project Obtuse" project, including the performance.

Daniel: Okay. That's the way I kind of understood it. But I just wanted to clarify. Ultimately, I've talked to Zach about his performance, so we don't have to go too much into that. But one of the things that came up in the Q&A afterwards was that Rachel from the Library Company discussed how there were these problematic materials held in their archives, and she said that the Library Company wanted to figure out how to share those materials with the broader public without causing harm. And so as a way to lead into "Beyond Glass Cases" more generally. I'm wondering if you could reflect a little bit about that goal for the Library Company and the museum field more generally?

Paul: I think the goal is important and an overdue one. I don't think that it's my place or within anybody's capacities at the present moment to state exactly how this should be done, because I think that thinking along the lines of this goal, trying to grapple with problematic archives and legacies and to present them to broad publics in ways that are sensitive, that don't reproduce harm, I think that's a matter that's not really been extensively applied or at the forefront of our thinking within museums and archives for very long or in many places. So, this is very much experimental. And I'm not so sure that we did everything correctly. I'm not so sure that this is the answer, but I do think it's an attempt, it's an honest attempt to try to find a way forward.

So I also think it's important that, I think it's really important as a gesture, and this doesn't answer your question, but it sort of outlines the scope of the problem. I think that one thing that institutions can do is try to hide this heritage, ignore it, which I think is a problem. And I think it's a problem in part because that very easily leads and accommodates a denial of these kinds of histories of racism, of exclusion, of marginalization that exists within the histories, archives, and collections. So how do you not ignore this material, and yet how do you display it in a way that is actually sensitive to the communities that are most impacted? And I think one of the most obvious first steps is to really include and center the voices of those people who are most impacted in the ways that you present this material.

It's a fundamental question of representation, and I think that's what we tried to do again as a first step with regard to this project. And I think it sets an important precedent that you don't talk about these histories of settler colonialism or scientific racism, for example, about Morton's "Crania Americana" in an exhibition without centering Indigenous voices in the way that story gets told. And I hope that is the precedent that this project sets, and that I think is really important and really exciting. It's about being open with regard to the fact this history exists and grappling honestly with the fact that maybe we don't have good or definitive answers about how to display these histories, how to show it, but setting a precedent that you don't do this without actually having a wider circle of people and diverse perspectives involved in how that's done, and particularly centering people most and directly impacted, in this case, Indigenous people. So I think that's important, and I think that's important as a white researcher working in this area. But I of course see a role for institutions and for researchers like myself who have deep expertise in these kinds of collaborations that bring these archives and bring expertise around them to broader communities, to also [be open to] different modalities of expression like artists to give these archives a voice and a life and to frame them with a perspective that we just haven't done in so much of museum and archival and collections practice.

Daniel: So that reminds me also of some of the other stated goals of the Library Company for this work. One of them was presenting these controversial

objects from their collection. Another one was sort of about exhibition strategies more generally and experimenting with them. And then also another
one was working with artists in terms of interpreting the materials. I guess
I'm just wondering what your impression is overall of these goals, how
you saw them interacting, if you feel like they were achieved through this
project? Were there other goals that you were bringing into your contribution
that were different from the ones that the Library Company was pursuing?

Paul: I'll say this. I think for me, I was really excited to have a chance to participate in something that was so different with regard to the way that these
histories were presented. And I will also note the Library Company is not
the only institution with a connection to Morton. There are other institutions
in Philadelphia that have Morton's papers, or are directly connected to his
legacy. I'll name three other big ones. One is the American Philosophical
Society. It has approximately the other half, maybe a little bit less of Morton's papers. The other is the Academy of Natural Sciences, which is now
part of Drexel University, which was where Morton worked, where he was
the president, where he amassed all of these skulls.

And then the third one is the Penn Museum that then accepted the skulls
from the Academy of Natural Sciences in the 1960s, first as a loan, then accessioned them in the 1990s. So the Penn Museum has housed these skulls
since the 1960s. All of these are problematic collections in ways of dealing
with Morton, and I've seen these institutions struggle particularly around the
human remains, but also with the archives themselves. And one of the ways
that institutions have tried to deal with this history is, explicitly or implicitly,
to skirt around it. The Library Company was willing to do something that
was really looking this history in the face, and being open about it, in a way
that some other institutions were not. So I was excited to be a part of it, and
I think that the success was being part of that precedent. It went beyond the
form of what we did. It was the precedent of acknowledging and foregrounding
the kind of ethical issues and the problematic history of these collections in
this kind of space. How we did it was one path through a very large space of
possibilities. It could have been different. So I was just excited to be a part
of that really kind of open and curious and honest approach to this history.

Daniel: Yeah. Well, I think some of the ways that they're thinking about it now
as the project wraps up, is not only what is the legacy of "Beyond Glass
Cases" for the Library Company internally, how does it inform the way that
they continue to do their work, but also relevance that the story of the project
can have for other peer institutions. And I think in particular at a moment

when institutions also might be pulling back from some of these impulses in some ways. So all that said, in closing, do you have further thoughts about lessons learned or advice for other institutions that are attempting to do similar kinds of work in their spaces and venues?

Paul: What I will say is this, and I say this very much from the perspective of a researcher, which has always been the primary hat I've really worn throughout this whole project, and that this kind of work really does illuminate collections in ways that more "traditional" modes of addressing and dealing with collections do not. And I think that, through this approach, there's real added value to the way that we understand these collections, relevant to the core missions of institutions trying to not just preserve but interpret history. This project actually did that for the Morton papers, and it did it in part through the kind of research that I did under its aegis, as it were. But it also did it by bringing in conversations and perspectives, like Zach's, that otherwise have long been excluded.

And frankly, I believe opening these archives to communities that otherwise would've had nothing to do with them or never would've heard of them. And I think that is an important part of what these kinds of critical projects can do, is, yeah, I think that if you're open to these conversations, if you don't shy away from them, it can not just illuminate collections and create better understanding [and] interpretation of the collections. It can make these collections meaningful to a much broader public. And I think in the long run, that is ultimately a good thing for everyone. I think that this path forward with this kind of critical and open and experimental approach, this is a way that can actually aid the fundamental missions of these institutions, many of which, including the Library Company, are wrestling with in the present moment, wrestling with how to connect with audiences. So I think that this is absolutely a way forward to meet the long-standing missions of these institutions and to advance academic research, but also increase their broader societal relevance. I think they need to embrace that.

Daniel: The way this manifests is contextually and culturally specific in the sense that the Library Company's version of this is going to be different than even the Penn Museum for a variety of reasons, just because of the culture and history of the institutions.

Paul: Of course, this will be different in different spaces. It may require its own specific kind of attention and intervention in each space. All of these require some scholarly groundwork. So, I've done, and I'm continuing to do, detailed scholarly work on Morton, scientific racism, and on "Crania Americana," and I think it's important. I think it's essential for that groundwork to be there. But I think that what this kind of project does is it gives an opportunity for that work to come alive to people for whom it would otherwise remain completely obscure. I mean, often I think there's also a lot of conversations that are parallel with regard to digitization of these archives. Because one of the matters is, and this is simplifying, but I think that one of the things that's interesting is that by digitizing these materials, you potentially widen their reach so much more broadly, and they kind of take on a life of their own, beyond the institution. And this is true with the Morton collection.

There are people who are becoming aware of this history and even inquiring about skulls in the collection because they've seen the digitized records online. They are being used in classrooms to teach history. Those records were always, in principle, publicly available. But through digitization, they're now, they can circulate through much more broadly. They're more accessible. And I think this is actually a kind of accessibility and the exact nature and what's happening here with these kinds of critical interventions. It's making these histories, these collections, these archives more accessible. How that will look is different in different contexts.

And the other thing I will just say, parenthetically, that was a really explicit decision with "Crania Americana and the Archive of Scientific Racism" or "Project Obtuse," was that we were focusing on how Morton's work related to settler colonialism. A big part of the rest of my work was really about the history of science and slavery. And that was essential to a lot of what else I've done about Morton, particularly as I was involved with the Penn and Slavery Project and with the Penn Program on Race, Science and Society focusing on those issues.

But it's not like we've done some kind of definitive project here with "Beyond Glass Cases" with regard to these archives. And I think that moving forward, there's going to be ways to expand this out to other communities and with other foci, also with other collections in the Library Company. So yeah, I think it's a fundamental shift in how these places work. What I like about the Library Company, is that this is an old institution and it wears its history very much on its sleeve, but it's also small enough to be flexible, experimental, to do something different.

That's what I really liked about this…that there are other places that wouldn't have been willing to take on the risks of a project like this one, but the Library Company was. We made something interesting happen as a result, and an important precedent. That kind of openness to approaching these histories in new ways is not only interesting, I think it is increasingly necessary to make these collections speak to broader audiences, and to the present moment.

"The Black Historians' Department: The Past Belongs to You" by Tafari Robertson

July 17, 2024–September 17, 2024

In "The Black Historians' Department: The Past Belongs to You," speculative historian Tafari Robertson created a space dedicated to the Black historians who cultivate their practice and stories outside of traditional institutions. It was a speculation of what would be different about history as a form if it were built around the ways that Black people hold and exchange information with each other and what it means to amplify and support those processes. Tafari explored these ideas with other members of Philadelphia's Black artistic and cultural community in a series of workshops/listening sessions. The exhibition that grew out of these sessions included an office setting and a living room interior setting where visitors were invited to engage with reference books, audio tapes, and video clips as ways to experience history. Two cases of items from the Library Company's African American History Collection were also displayed. "The Past Belongs to You" was an invitation to understand Black history as a community practice, not to be discovered or authorized, but participated in.

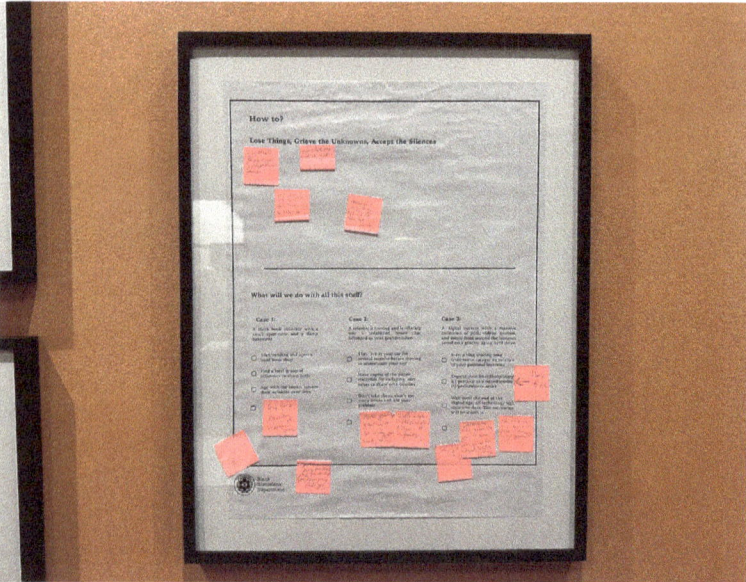

SALON

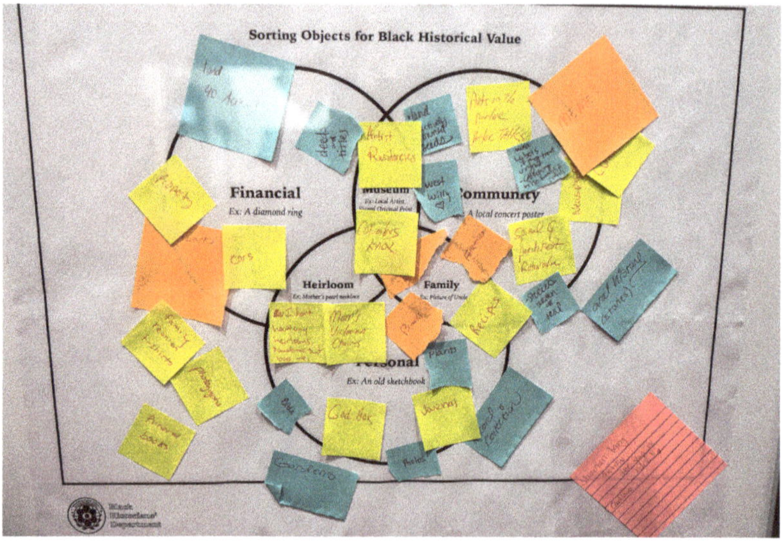
Sorting Objects for Black Historical Value
Financial
Ex: A diamond ring
A local concert poster
Heirloom
Family
Ex: An old sketchbook

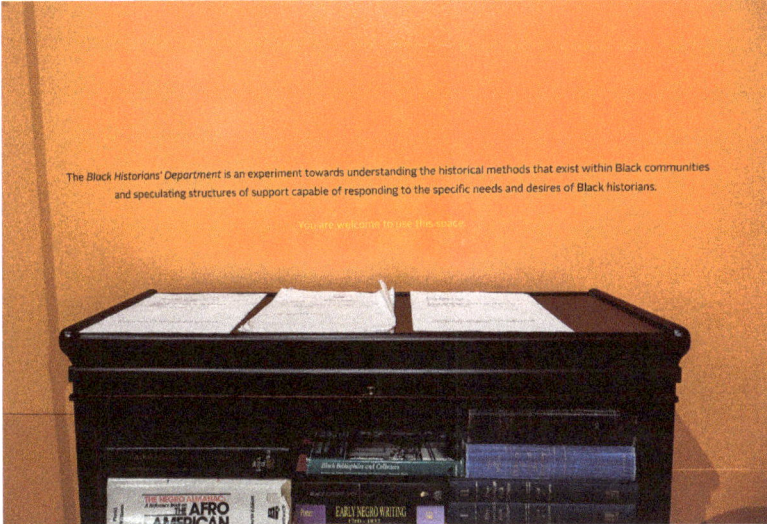

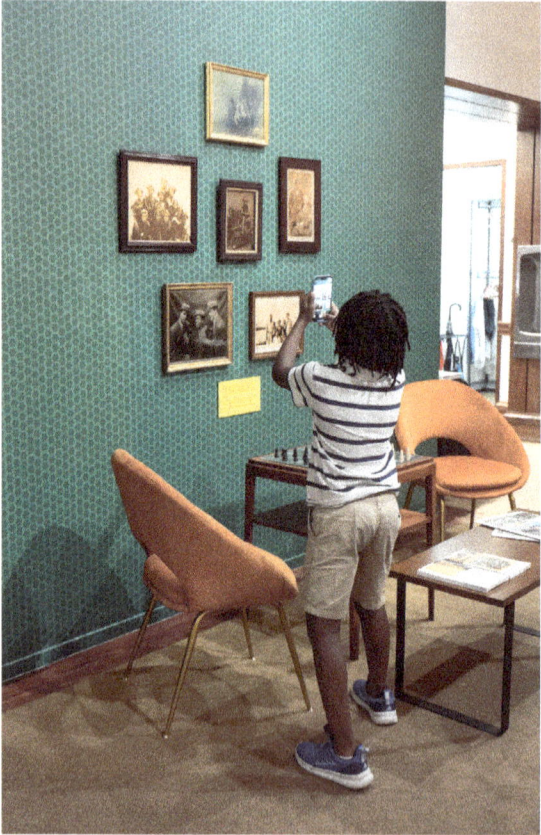

Interview: Tafari Robertson

This interview was conducted by Daniel Tucker on May 1, 2025.

Daniel: I was wondering if you could share a little bit about the pre-history of your project "The Black Historians' Department?" Obviously your engagement with history precedes this work with the Library Company. So could you offer a little bit more context for maybe one experience that really made you think about the value of independent community-based archiving and history writing that ultimately informed this project?

Tafari: Well, I've been [doing] community work since I was in high school and middle school even, actually. And I worked at a history museum. I'm from Texas, and I worked with Kenny Dorham's Backyard, which is a historical blues venue, run by Harold McMillan. And the Calaboose African American History museum in San Marcos. So basically I've just been a part of winning this struggle of trying to make space for Black history, trying to preserve it, and the challenges of doing it in these grassroots ways and the lack of institutional support in a lot of ways that impact the ability to preserve in a more structural way, but also the people work that goes into keeping it alive.

I also worked with the Paul Robeson House [here in Philadelphia, which helped me realize the importance of how] this only exists because of Fran Aulston doing a grassroots effort to bring people from her community together and then passing the torch. And so Vernoca keeping it alive, Chris Rogers bringing a new generation in and so on and so forth. So it is always this effort of people working together to keep major histories alive that otherwise people wouldn't know about. So that's the institutional history, but also just as an artist, I've been interested in Black conceptual art and space and doing assemblages and installations, so it comes naturally to me.

Daniel: Well, continuing with that, I'm wondering what ended up being the genesis of your involvement with "Beyond Glass Cases?" How did you get brought into that process?

Tafari: Definitely. It's actually right in a similar vein. My friend and my colleague, Wynn Eakins, worked at the Library Company as the African American history specialist in the reading room. Wynn told me about this project, encouraged me to apply, and so I submitted my application, and then Wynn initially was the advisor for my project as well. Well, Emily Guthrie was the first advisor, but then, well, inside the Library Company there, a lot of changing hands. So Wynn ultimately moved on to another job, but there was a period of time where Wynn was my liaison, I guess is the word, my liaison to the Library Company. Not advisor, but liaison.

But basically I'm just saying it's like, it's very similar in the sense of I actually was not really aware of the Library Company before this. I'm pretty new to this style of art-making that is grant funding and institutionally involved in this way. So it was really the relationship to Wynn that brought me into this at all. So that also I felt was important to reflect when I was thinking about my project and thinking about just again, the work of Black history, how there is a relational aspect that doesn't get the official credit because it's supposed to be just off of merit. But the merit, I mean, we are all really skilled. There's a lot of really skilled artists and historians around the city who don't have any relationship to the Library Company in Philadelphia.

Daniel: Right. Well, continuing with that relational orientation, I'm thinking about something that I heard you say or read that you wrote—I can't remember. That your project was premised on history, that it is created and it's a process done by people, and that because of those people being involved, we have as much access to recreate it as well as participate in this creation. And you also later said, speaking of the relational aspect that you want to "study your friends, you want to quote them, you want to write them down." So I'm wondering if you could share a little bit about how this approach to history relates to things that you encountered at the Library Company. Did you see that kind of relationality in the materials that you saw there? Was that what sort of inspired you to make that emphasis? Or was it a reaction? Was it not found in the kinds of historical materials that were there and you wanted to do something different that had this kind of dimension to it?

Tafari: Well, the idea actually started because I applied for the "Beyond Glass Cases" project that ultimately Mark Thomas Gibson did, but responding to the "Liberty Displaying the Arts and Sciences" painting and so my application was really about looking at this painting and asking these questions of what happens to this painting that is really non-historical? So what is this process of looking at these old classical paintings? What happens to them to make them worthy of not only consideration in the first place, but then reconsideration when we're looking at these things that are challenging or they've changed in terms of their problematicness. But I was just looking at that and being like, but this is not a historical event, it's just the painting that a person did. So was it because he was rich? Was it because he had a relationship to somebody? What was it? What happened to this painting that made it different from any other person that did a painting?

So that was originally where the idea started from, as far as what I was proposing to the Library Company, [it] was this critique and investigation into what makes things historical and what happens if you give those powers of authority to Black people, basically. But it was specifically looking at the response to that, because I was thinking about being like, this is only here because someone gave this to whatever Benjamin Franklin or something. And then a lot of times in terms of the Library Company institution is really built on the relationships of, well, this was Benjamin Franklin's collection, and then he exchanged hands with these other white people who had resources and power to create a value system over time that we're still honoring in terms of this collecting process. But specifically thinking about the Philadelphia, W.E.B. Du Bois went to the Library Company to study for the "Philadelphia Negro" project back in the 1900s, that's one of his most famous works, W.E.B. Du Bois.

Daniel: Yeah, I didn't know that he used the Library Company as a source.

Tafari: And there's no record or any evidence or anything about one of the leading Black social scientists, historians, and activists having this experience or this relationship to the Library Company in Philadelphia.

So I'm just saying that as a comparison: here's a painter who, or all these paintings all around this building, all this literature, all throughout this building of wealthy white people that is preserved kind of as a testament to their wealth and the decisions that they were able to make because of that. But in a city that has been predominantly Black and has such an impact on the world that has been made by the Black people from Philadelphia. And you're very hard-pressed to find any of that history inside the Library Company without an extensive amount of digging a very specific layer of research. And I don't mean that to say that as a specific disrespect to the Library Company. That's just true of history.

So even knowing Black history at all relies on our relationship to each other because it's just not upheld institutionally. The resources just simply aren't there. And even the history of moments where it has been, there is a history of it being contested constantly. So I think that's why I say history is this opportunity for people. I'm thinking specifically about Black people as marginalized and marginalized people in general as something where the majority of the way we learn about history, the way we receive history has been dictated to us from external sources. What is the process that happens?

What is making a decision that this is something that's important to us that is worth preserving? And where does that actually happen?

Daniel: I'm wondering, in your initial proposal, did you frame it as this Black Historians' Department? Was that the way that you conceptualized it, and was it in any way in dialogue with the Library Company's program in African American history?

Tafari: No, it came to be the Black Historians' Department through conversations. I started out with salons that I had in the Cassat House with my friends who I, I'm very, very excited and privileged for myself [that] my peers are already archeologists and historians and artists and curators. So that was something where I was very intentional about making a space to bring people in who were already my thought partners, just in my relationships.

But through that process is where it became the Black Historians' Department, which actually was a distinction that was a shift from this kind of history-making, and is it Black history? It's Black historians. There was a lot that we were kind of mulling over. We mulled over a lot. There was some challenges to it, even being called a department because of…what are you playing with in terms of your suggestion of authority and institutional control that is implied by department. So those things were shifted around, but more so in relationship to my community of peers and us coming into this space and investigating things together, less than in real relationship to the Library Company or the African American specialist department.

But it's interesting because even in the Library Company, while I was working on my project, there were a lot of institutional changes. I didn't have a strong relationship to the person, but I just know that while I was working, the African American department was run by a Black woman at some point, and was laid off, and now it's run by a white man. And so that's happening before I even really got a chance to talk to her, involve her in my process, and whatever the relationship was to the Library Company as an institution, I didn't get a chance to get into the weeds of that or know what might have been set up. So again, there's things that happened behind the scenes, and I'm not wanting to expose or share anyone else's personal business, but I'm just saying from outside looking in, it's like, oh, having someone to talk to as an access point of being like, okay, a Black historian handling Black history.

But often inside the institutions, that's such a fragile position. But that's really important because that's what would've brought me to talk to someone to say, oh, what is the Library Company's actual relationship to the historical materials that you have? But fortunately, Wynn was also a specialist, and that was my peer. So I spent most of my relationship to the materials of the Library Company was supported by Wynn, and then going to the print room, with Sarah [Weatherwax], and also working with Ms. Sharon [Hildebrand], but the point is—I didn't actually have a strong relationship to the Library Company materials in the development of my project. I mostly spent the time working through the idea of what are Black historians doing?

Daniel: Yeah. Well, even as you talk a little bit about the naming, I think it's compelling to frame it as a department, but where the emphasis of what the department is focused on is not necessarily Black History, but it's Black Historians where the actual focus of the department is the people. I think that it's a useful way that you set that up through the naming and then it's reinforced throughout all your decisions to highlight these friendship and peer networks that are so important to your work. So to give you a chance to talk a little bit more about the shape of what you ended up doing, as I under-stand it, your project ultimately kind of had these three parts, an exhibition, some programming that was closed, and then some programming that was open to the public, including this variety show called a Black Speculative History course. But could you talk me through those three elements and some of the shape of them?

Tafari: Yeah, definitely. So that actually was one of the through lines from some of the earlier ideas of the project, which was creating this series of processes where I'm asking throughout—where does something become historical? Where does the historical event kind of land? Is it when you talk about it? So in this "salon," is it when we get together or we make decisions? So out of those conversations, I made documents that I would use [at events] such as these questionnaires and surveys concerned with where does something get to be history? Is it in the presentation to people? Is it in the sharing? And doing the variety show and doing another salon—I invited, again, a wider network of the people who I knew to come in and for Black people to come in and get to be in a space of making decisions. So the charts that I had up in my exhibition are from that roundtable, just literally just putting the charts down on the table, feeding people, playing some music and just saying, just talk to each other. See what happens. There isn't an informational science or allegiance that I'm enforcing. I want to see what people are drawn to. I want to see what draws out these bits of information. And these are the questions that came up from the salons that we had in a series of private sessions.

And then finally there was the installation. So following that was an intentional segmenting of where along a process of this sort of creation does the decision to make something historical become real? So that was something that was a through line from the original question of what makes history, who gets to make history, and [whether we] are allowed to do it. That then got folded into the idea to "Black Historians' Department." Originally I was applying for the "library sciences" project, but they suggested or sort of redirected my project to the "community choice" project. So it kind of opened it up.

That allowed for me to be like, okay, well fine. If I don't have to deal with any central object that is dictated to me, then I'm really free to open this question up. Just to this question of Black historians and also with the events and all these processes, a lot of the challenges taking an environment that is otherwise kind of inconsiderate and not just in a rude way, but sometimes, but an environment that is just not really in consideration of Black experience inside the space—as far as navigating information and what is the sort of popular experience...and I'm not saying this as a specific dig to the Library Company; I'm just saying this as an archive and these sort of academic sort of silent-one style of research spaces. You're expected to come in and sit down and know what you're talking about and get your head into a book and just move independently. That's the style of research that we're brought into. If you go to academia, to grad school, it's like you are working on a paper. So you'll go to a special collection, you'll find a certain material, and you'll just sort of bury your nose and be quiet.

So a big and exciting challenge of every step of my process was how do I undo some of that? How do I acknowledge another process happening where we're learning because we can eat together. We're learning because we can talk and we can make noise and we can laugh. How do I transform the reading room that specifically demands that you be quiet and in respect of other scholars, which is whatever, but doing an event in that space and making it a space that is an event. It's lively. It's about mingling. And I know I'm not the only person to do events, that they have events all the time, but I wanted to make people kind of forget where they were. I wanted to bring Black people into a space and forget that there are these kind of eerie paintings of old white people looking down on you.

So as an artist, this is where I get into [my influence from] conceptual artists. It's like also what makes a space? What is this institutional engagement? What is engagement that allows people to open up and talk to each other? What are those elements? Where does the money go? What does it mean to bring in peers? And how does that create security and comfort for people to go to a space that they otherwise maybe never even considered entering? That never felt welcoming.

Daniel: I got to watch the recording from the variety show, and it seemed like you created a really exciting and fun program. So I hope that people were able to feel that kind of shift that you set up.

Tafari: Yeah, that one was exciting because again, I know these people, and I know that they have really, really cool personal interests and sense of information, and they were friends, they were people I worked with. I was considering, what does it take to get to a space where you are allowed to be presenting at a place like the Library Company? Typically it would mostly be professors or grad students or scholars in some regard. Part of the consideration was, "I know you know what you're talking about, and I just want you to trust yourself and get to step behind this podium in a place that would probably in any other circumstance, that never really acknowledge that you are the holder of this history."

One of the presenters, Sherry (Howard) did her presentation on the Black arts community movement of Philadelphia in the 1980s and 1990s into the early 2000s, and who were the key artists and who were just very on the ground work, who was a person who's approaching as a journalist, but also has been working and invested in that community, how to approach auctions. So an aboveground under the ground process. But again, that is such valuable information. [It's the] same as, [saying] this person has this relationship to Philadelphia, and this is their definition of this route and these museums, and this is how they navigate the city. So that was really fun to do. That was really fun to do.

Daniel: Something you mentioned in some of your documents was that there's all this important Black history that is untapped because it doesn't focus on traumatic events or around people's celebrity, but it's kind of more grounded in, I think, something that's, as you phrased it "starts with selfhood." And so I found it a really effective process that you used these questionnaires—where you gave everyone the same questions to respond to as a thread to connect all the presentations. I wrote the questions down: "How do you remember the places or people best? What's the last thing you got? What's the last thing you got that you want to keep forever and how will you make sure you do, and where do histories happen that go unnoticed by formal institutions?" So I'm wondering if you could talk a little bit more about, I think you mentioned that some of those questions came from your salons that you were organizing. Is that right? And just talk a little bit about how the presenters ended up responding to it.

Tafari: Yeah, the questions I wrote and I sent it to them in advance when I was inviting them to perform and give their presentations. So yeah, I mean, the questions [were] really just something that I just came up with. It was all a part of this creating this well of knowledge. So what we talked about in some of the salons was—what are the other institutional or organizational efforts around these same themes? And just kind of challenging each other as peers to say, well, have you considered this? Or, oh, here's some books that I've been inspired by. What do y'all think about this? That was a lot of what was happening, and along that led to me making some of the forms that I made and the charts that I made, the questions themselves were definitely a part of that.

I [was also] literally looking around my apartment and being like, how do we end up with some of the things that we have? Another big part of [my process] was my family and going through an old photo album and realizing my dad has a photo album, and in one of the pictures, it's just a picture of a table. When I was looking at this book, then it occurred to me that it was like, oh, yeah, we've had this table since I was a child. And I was asking my mom, I was like, why would you just have a picture of a table? Every other picture is a picture of a family, and it really is just a flash photo of this table. And I was like, maybe it's just a test photo. So I'm like, maybe this is a photo that represents, oh, this is when you first got this camera. Maybe this photo represents this. And she's like, oh, I don't know. It might've been the first table that your dad got in our first apartment or something. But again, being like, oh, so this wasn't, again, this process as something that wasn't initially deemed historical. But here, this process has had subconsciously between this picture and the time, where I'm like, now I'm like, oh, I guess this is an important table. This might be something I need to keep.

So anyway, I'm just saying that as what prompted this idea of the question "what was the last object that you got that you're going to keep forever and how you're going to keep it?" Because I was thinking both about how this happens subconsciously, but how much also gets lost? Because when we are experiencing these big moments of loss, or we have to move or we become displaced or anything, that sorting has to happen on a dime. And so a lot of really important things can get lost. Someone passes away and they have a basement full of things that they were keeping forever, but we don't have any documentation of why they kept certain things. So that's just the thought process of that one question. I think all the questions were similarly probing of how do you get to an understanding of a historical practice that's happening that everyone is participating in, whether they are a formally considered historian or not.

Daniel: Yeah, that's really helpful. Thanks. Well, so I'm wondering more generally about "Beyond Glass Cases" as a project. It had these, a couple of different goals in mind. One was about, which you already talked about a little bit, kind of controversial objects. One was about experimenting with exhibition strategies and approaches, and then the other one was about the role of artists and the potential for them to be involved in interpreting materials in the collection, making them relevant to different contemporary conversations. So I'm wondering just if you could talk about how you experienced the overall project across those goals and how you saw them interact and to what extent those were at all brought into your own contribution or if you brought in other different goals that exceeded what they were focused on with "Beyond Glass Cases?"

Tafari: I realized at multiple points throughout it that my project was really ambitious as far as the work and what I was doing as far as bringing people together and hosting events. It always comes together and it's really fun, but I kind of stockpile a lot of work onto myself. I don't really have an assistant or anything like that. So all the designs for all of the events, I did all of the event planning. I did hire my friend A'jon who was also really helpful as an events specialist to help me with communication and just straight up setup and things like that—it was really valuable to have their help. And so yeah, I brought my friends into the process to help me and to support me more so as a buffer also to my relationship to the Library Company.

And like I said, the experience of entering this archive is like you come in, if you say you're interested in Black history, they're going to present to you. They have a book full of old cartoons and illustrations that are put into their Black collection, and it's just minstrelsy and lynching and just terrorism. So if you go in and you type in Black on the website, if you go in and you start truly from scratch, if you're going in just interested, you have to get through a lot of painful sludge before you can start navigating to what you're interested in. And again, a lot of scholars come through who are already very experienced and very skilled in navigating these sorts of special collections. They're not doing that same process. They have a special interest and a time period, and they're looking for these letters and these correspondences. And I've learned honestly, more from starting from that process and now with some of the work that I'm doing, [that] there's sort of a side door of approaching special collections and research that you wouldn't necessarily know about if you're approaching it as you would approach a public library being like, "oh, well, do you have anything on Black history?" That is a way, but that's going to create a much more complicated relationship than if you are like, "I'm looking for what was happening in South Philadelphia from 1898 to 1901. Do you have any letters?" That's a different thing that I'm learning more and more as I engage with these kinds of collections.

I think of my piece as an institutional critique. So when I created my installation, finally what became my exhibition, it was again about creating a space where people can get comfortable having these conversations, considering ourselves. So putting a table, putting a couch, putting a desk area where it's like, it was almost like tongue-in-cheek to me where I'm like, oh, yeah, they'll come into the formal receptionist desk and then you turn and there's another desk, and it's like, well, what's this? Where previously that's just gallery space that's traditionally just for being walked through. And then we also hosted office hours and more salons and activated that exhibition space. Again, bringing in people who otherwise don't have time or aren't interested or aren't in a grad program or aren't anything that is going to narrow a research focus for you specifically that gives you a reason to go to the Library Company.

So creating a "Black Historians' Department" inside of the Library Company was, I think, a critique of the fact that we deserve our own spaces. We don't have a Black archive institution in Philadelphia. And so carving this space is inherently a critique of, yeah, there isn't a space for this kind of research. There isn't acknowledgment of this kind of research that otherwise has to happen in living rooms and parks and maybe some parts of the public library—but even that is very threatened as far as places where you just get to gather and get to become comfortable enough to spend time with your special interests.

Daniel: As a final question, I'm wondering if you have any "lessons learned" not only for the Library Company, but also for their peer institutions more generally that might be attempting to do kind of similar projects or ask similar questions again, around exhibition strategies, around working with artists, and around contextualizing controversial objects? Do you have any reflections from your experience about that might kind of be lessons learned for the field more generally?

Tafari: Definitely. Absolutely. Especially because like I said, there was a high [staff] turnover while I was working on my project. So that is one as far as, especially for the people working on and now we see in America in general, the people who were supporting and facilitating these parts of this process and bringing the people together were the most at risk. The people who were very intentional about taking care of me and meeting needs and supporting, not in any even special way, but just actually helping my events see through helping me communicate and connect dots that I didn't know about were the people who felt the most on edge throughout my process because of the changing climate both institutionally and globally.

So that was one I felt at different points I had to be, even getting an opportunity to do such a project of this scale felt a little bit like snuck in. I don't have a master's degree. I'm not from a formal institution that gave me a lot of experience with this style of grant writing. And I feel like my project was really, really successful and brought in a lot of people, and by all accounts and all measures, especially if they're talking about how do we get new people to engage with these spaces.

So I think I was successful in my goals, but I also think I was very successful in their goals, even though my goals were kind of intentionally in disregard of their goals. So I feel like the big lessons learned was about halfway through the project, there's this question of like, oh, I'm doing a lot of work for an institution that I couldn't get hired at, credentially speaking. And I think that happens a lot with moments where artists are coming in to reflect and do work on special collections, and there are these temporary things and artists are in these very tentative positions in general because we work on a grant to grant basis. We hop from institution to institution.

So that's not me saying "hire me," but I think that was just an interesting part of this experience of us doing all of this programming and all of this. I sort of took that liberty, but it still is, if institutions are looking to do this sort of critical work, I think it would be really important for them to take seriously the amount of energy that brings to the space, the different energy that it brings to this space. And I think it's important for it to happen because like I said, there are so many artists, especially Black artists, historians, historically-engaged, and culturally-engaged people all around the city who never even consider opportunities like this. They just never have been invited. And for me, it took, literally, an invitation. I never would've applied for the Library Company history grant just as a person browsing. I don't know how it ever would've even ended up on the Library Company's website if it hadn't been because of my relationship to Wynn.

But comparing that to what I felt like was very successful work that brought in all of the events were packed. Not a single event was sparse. So it was successful, but that required me being brought in and made to feel welcome. And so I would, for the institutions that are more reinforced in this era, as all of the arts institutions and historical and cultural institutions are being threatened, we know for a fact that Black history is specifically those [kinds of] institutions that are going to be threatened first.

So I think for people who may be reading this publication, it would be really important for them to consider those invitations and not just in the sort of fragile, temporary bolstering-your-marketing-campaign or whatever, but what does it actually mean to expand that stability to Black artists and Black historians?

There is an organization called the Black Docents Collective that works in Philadelphia, and they are a product of a [group] of docents from the African American Museum. And frankly, it's a collective of elders who do a lot of embedded historical work at all these institutions, whether they're docents or whether they're just personal patrons, whatever. But there was an interesting moment while I was doing my speech at my opening and looking at these people who came to support this project and came to talk to me about this project and kind of knowing like,

Oh, you're an institution too. You are the president of a Black Docents collective that is meeting at the library and meeting in people's houses and meeting in these fragile nomadic ways that has no funding...Or, you are the president of this Black archive community that is doing genealogical work, that is actually doing the tracing of the Underground Railroad from here to here and doing cemetery work, and you have no funding.

But I am in this position of like, oh, "I've received this funding for my conceptual project inside of an institution that's reinforced by dominant funding, but the Black institutions that are doing this long legacy work are mostly upheld by small fringe community groups that have no funding."

So I think [a lesson is] being very intentional about connecting that infrastructural support to organizations like that and not doing the handholding or patronizing as much as being like, you know what you're doing, because that was the thing that I also needed. I was just a person. There's a certain amount that I still experience every time I do work with a bigger institution of being like, Hey, there's some unspoken deadlines that will make your life a little easier. You're allowed to ask for help here.

Actually, a big moment for me was trying to figure out how to do my installation. That was at the end of my project, inside of my budget for what I had received through this grant. And it was very important, even though it was small for Ms. Sharon [Hildebrand], the conservator at the Library Company to explain to me like, "oh, we actually have a budget for installations. I have a budget that we use for sustaining our gallery, so that's not something you need to worry about." Just that thing completely shifted what I would've been able to accomplish with some of my funding, because a lot of us are coming from a DIY grassroots way [of working].

So I was thinking, "okay, which of my friends has a truck? How am I going to find these materials on Facebook marketplace to stock this official gallery?" And so those are things that when we're working with people who are not inside the institution, are really, really helpful to lay out. There's a lot of unspoken understood things, and I think a lot of people who have bad experiences with this kind of work, because there isn't someone to tell them that, "oh, we actually cover this. We actually have funds for this. You actually aren't responsible for all of your marketing. We actually have a marketing department. Oh, we actually have infrastructural support that people are just simply not used to having."

So I think that was the biggest learning thing that I would want the institutions to really take into consideration.

Daniel: I think that's super helpful and generous advice from your experience.

SECTION 3

Behind The Scenes

Images: Photos from "Reflections" Exhibition on View from
March 18, 2025 to July 3, 2025

Interview: Emily Guthrie
and Sarah Weatherwax

Former Library Company of Philadelphia Librarian Emily Guthrie served as "Beyond Glass Cases" Project Manager from the beginning of the grant in October 2022 until her departure from the Library Company in March 2024. Senior Curator of Graphic Arts Sarah Weatherwax took over this role for the remainder of the grant

This interview was conducted by Daniel Tucker on March 24, 2025.

Daniel: I think that it would be helpful for me, and I think also readers of this publication who want to understand the scope of the project, to think a little bit about the prehistory of "Beyond Glass Cases." And obviously the prehistory, if you think about the history of the Library Company is very long. But to pull back, say, five years or so and think about, what kinds of things in the years prior to "Beyond Glass Cases" were being discussed internally within the Library Company? My sense from just being in the field in Philly is there's a pretty long history of the Library Company doing exhibitions on progressive topics and questions and themes. So that wasn't necessarily the innovation of "Beyond Glass Cases." But can you talk a little bit about any maybe key projects or key conversations that this might've been built on?

Emily: So I arrived at the Library Company in April of 2021. So I wasn't there five years ago, but I was certainly included in the origins of "Beyond Glass Cases." So what was going on when I arrived was we had a director named Mike Barsanti, who I think had been there for just about five years when I arrived. And he hired me. And then during my hiring process and in my early time there, he talked a lot about the Library Company's exhibition program and how he felt like it needed a refresh. I had been an admirer of the Library Company's exhibition program for a long time. I was working not too far away from Philadelphia, so I was on the mailing list and getting all the updates and all of that. And I always thought that, wow, what a great place. They're taking on interesting topics and seemed to have really positive response. So I was kind of surprised that the director felt like the exhibition program needed a refresh, and his concerns were that the program was too expensive. I think we had a budget of, I'm remembering about $20,000 a year. So pretty low really compared to other libraries and that it took, exhibitions really took up too much of the staff time, depending on the exhibition. I think curators could have about three years to prepare and that…

Sarah: …Yeah, I think it depends on how proactive the curator was in proposing a topic and how open the schedule. I mean, the Library Company has never been great about having a long-term exhibition schedule in place. We've gotten a little better over the years, but it's not something that three to five years out we've necessarily gotten in order. It would be just the next couple of years when we presumably knew what we were doing.

Emily: Yeah. And I guess a lot of those timelines were dictated by grants as well. So a lot of the exhibitions had some sort of grant component or grant support, and he also observed that exhibition attendance was generally low. He was really big on the Library Company being seen as innovative and in innovation—the words he used a lot. He wanted us to be innovative in our approach to everything. So exhibitions, our programs and events, and then these awards that we give out. So he thought that we could apply the same sort of level of innovation to our exhibition program, perhaps in that moment, not fully recognizing how innovative the Library Company really already was with the topics that they took on and how they were being recognized amongst our peers. So that was one component.

I think [we were] still working through the impact of all of the events of the pandemic and certainly the impact on public events and programming online versus in person, as well as the events of 2020 and the library. You remember how all the places were making commitments to DEI and the Library Company had a really good one. And so I think we were still working through those commitments and efforts to diversify the staff, the board, and to reach a more diverse audience.

[And there was] also the big thing happening with the Samuel Jennings "Liberty Displaying the Arts and Sciences" painting. And so I'm not sure how much of the backstory you've heard on that…

Daniel: Well, I know about the painting and I've seen it, and I just in fact talked to Mark Thomas Gibson, of course, for an hour about it. But that said, I don't know what kind of conversations were happening internally about those objects.

Sarah: Do you want me…?

Emily: …To jump in on that one, Sarah?

Sarah: Yeah. The conversation Emily is just referring to is the Samuel Jennings painting, "Liberty Displaying the Arts and Sciences," which was displayed in the first floor reading room for years and years and years. It became a lightning rod when there was some staff pushback against having a painting, which is viewed by many people to be racist, who felt uncomfortable with that painting as literally looming over them as they did research or visited the Library Company since that was a space that a lot of our lectures and other events took place in as well. So the painting was moved to another location on the first floor. And that became, I think, to our director's surprise, a very controversial thing to do. There was a lot of pushback from many of our long-term shareholders who didn't understand why the painting offended or upset researchers and the staff.

And [after that] there were some, I believe Michael Barsanti, our former director, called them Family and Friends Conversations.

Emily: Yes, that's right.

Sarah: Friends.

Emily: And family.

Sarah: Friends and Family, depending on who you want to put first. I guess that attempted to have a discussion, a respectful discussion, where differing opinions could be expressed, and it did not go well. And I think there were a lot of hurt feelings. There was a lot of anger. Board members sort of took sides as to whether this painting should be in the reading room, because it's very intertwined with the Library Company's history, so how you view the painting became sort of a lightning rod for I think a lot of the bigger issues that were going on in the outside world as well as internally at the Library Company.

Daniel: Thanks for that, Sarah. And maybe before we move on to "Beyond Glass Cases," Sarah, I know your history goes back further than Emily's at the Library Company, and so I'm just wondering if you could fill in any other context in terms of the exhibitions program, pivotal or catalytic projects, or conversations in addition to the ones that have already been mentioned?

Sarah: Yeah, I mean, I would certainly agree with Emily's take that the Library Company, I thought had done a pretty good job of being, I'm very tired of the word innovative, but innovative with our exhibitions. I know in the grant, the "Beyond Glass Cases" grant application to Pew two exhibits were kind of specifically highlighted. One was "Ghost River," which I think that took place…[in] 2019 to 2020…which was Pew-funded and [took on] the narrative about the Paxton Boys massacre of indigenous people in Lancaster County and flipped it to the indigenous perspective and worked with the indigenous community on curating the exhibition and doing a graphic novel.

"Imperfect History" was an exhibition from 2021, which really kind of critically examined the 50th anniversary of the founding of the graphic arts department within the Library Company. We wanted to do something that wasn't necessarily celebratory, but was just sort of an honest evaluation of how the graphics collection evolved, who thought it was important to collect what or to not collect certain things and why. So I did feel like we were on a path of internally starting to question some of our own history, or at least examine it with a critical eye. [And also] looking for other topics like, "Common Touch," which was reaching out to the low-vision community and working with artists about ways of dealing and interacting with the collections.

So yeah, I'm a little surprised that that's what Mike felt was something that we weren't doing well. There are many things I could have pointed out that I didn't think we were doing well, but actually our exhibitions [were working well], other than they were very time-consuming in terms of the staff, and we don't get a huge audience. So I think that to me has always been sort of the tension with the exhibitions program [that is] how much staff time should be spent on something and what is our hope for the exhibitions program? Is it driving a lot of people in here, or is it somehow reaching them through other ways beyond what's actually in the gallery?

Emily: Can I add just a couple other things that I think were going on in that moment? A couple of other pressure points. At the time, we were relying heavily on grant funding to kind of balance the Library Company's budget and to subsidize staff salaries. And so the more grants the better, and we were applying for grants not necessarily out of a need to fund a specific project that was coming from a staff interest in fulfilling that project as much as it was to find funding to help our bottom line, to be frank. So there was a development officer at the Library Company at the time who was truly just applying for every opportunity that we could. So there was a lot of just pressure on the staff at that time to play along with these grant opportunities.

Daniel: Yeah. Well, that makes sense. And maybe also is another way to read between the lines of commentary like "innovative exhibitions," because it may not be a reflection of the quality of the exhibitions as much as the funding stream, the access to funding streams that are tied to different perceptions of innovation. Building on that, I think that my read on some of the other goals of "Beyond Glass Cases" was that it was multifaceted—that there were multiple goals. That one was about controversial objects in the collection. One was about exhibition strategies more generally, literally what you, what's said in the name "Beyond Glass Cases," and then finally about the potential of using artists to interpret the collection. And so I guess

I'm wondering if you all could talk a little bit about the balance that was envisioned across these goals? Maybe anything further about how they came about, if you think there were other goals that I am not understanding about the project and how you envisioned they might interact with one another?

Sarah: Yeah, I mean, certainly the idea of working with artists to interpret the collection is not anything new to the library. So while I think that was put forth as "isn't this an exciting opportunity?," it really wasn't particularly innovative. We'd been doing it for a good number of years. So in my mind, that wasn't that important a goal because I thought we had already sort of started to make those connections and had those opportunities and had for, at that point, probably at least a decade, worked with artists and others.

I felt like the goal that might have been one of the more worthwhile goals, but was one that didn't pan out very well, was how what we learned through "Beyond Glass Cases" would apply to future exhibition strategies. And I think that became a bit of the lack of seeming commitment from an institutional perspective for what "Beyond Glass Cases" was about, that was one of its great weaknesses. It was very hard to get staff behind and apparently the board and others behind "Beyond Glass Cases" because there really wasn't a plan for how we would continue in the vein of "Beyond Glass Cases" with future exhibitions. It seemed very performative for a lot of people, and I think focusing on controversial objects, it was not very clear in the grant other than the Jennings painting was mentioned and the Samuel Morton papers. But other than that, it was very murky who would be defining what was controversial, and I think that was a core weakness of the project as well.

Emily: Yeah, this question was a tough one for me. As I was thinking about how I would answer this, I'm not sure that "balance" was envisioned across these goals. The project had a lot of goals. It seemed like a good way to max out the funding opportunity, and I think when they were writing the grant, they imagined three easy steps. The first one would be that the library staff would have an opportunity to work with an external consulting group to prepare ourselves better to work with harmful objects and find new and different ways to interpret these objects to the public. Something we already had experimented with and done fairly well, but there's always [room] for growth there, and how do we engage new audiences by finding different ways to talk about these things and demonstrate, perhaps performatively, that we're not hiding these things away. We're ready to keep these harmful objects in the conversation.

So we were supposed to work with this external group to build language and skills around this approach. That was step phase one. Phase two would be three rapid fire prototype experiences, which was the term that the director developed for this kind of experimental approach that he wanted to use to find new ways of presenting objects outside of the object-in-a-case-with-label model. But figuring out what a prototype experience was and having enough time to do that type of work was a real challenge. So we scrapped that prototype experience model pretty quickly after we found out we got the grant. And then third, it was supposed to be wrapped up with "Hey, what did you learn? Let's present it to the public and wrap it up neatly, we learned these things and call it done." So yeah, I guess we were supposed to find balance among those three steps, and they were supposed to be neatly in sequence [as if] everything falls into place. But it's quite complicated.

Sarah: And I think clearly anyone who's actually done curatorial work would scoff at that as the timeline and the framework for this project. It just wasn't sustainable from the get-go as far as I was concerned. There wasn't time built in to actually think about any lessons to create something that demonstrates those lessons. I don't know. I found it to be an ill-conceived project.

Daniel: Maybe to drill into it a little bit more, I know from talking to Sarah a little bit that things didn't work out originally with the consultant that you wrote into the grant application. But can you tell me a little bit more about the process that did unfold? I mean, what kind of internal conversations, if any, did you have about working with these objects and how were they facilitated?

Sarah: You [Emily] probably know more than I do about that. I mean, from my perspective, when the original consulting firm was part of this project, I was not particularly part of the project. So I can speak to it as just a staff member at the Library Company, not a "Beyond Glass Cases" team member. The firm came to the Library Company and met, I think individually with every staff member. I think just kind of talking about the culture at the Library Company, I don't specifically remember. And then we had an all-staff meeting where we broke into I think smaller groups to discuss maybe a few questions. But again, it seemed very nebulous to me. But I think the consulting firm, I think was supposed to meet with the board. But correct me if I'm wrong, I don't think that ever happened, Emily.

Emily: That did not happen. So the original consulting firm was hired because they were recommended by a board member, I'll say that, who had a professional connection to them. They were very far away. One of them lived in

California; another lived in Washington State. So all of our initial meetings with them were done online. And then I think I scheduled, I don't know, at least two full days' worth of in-person workshops with them. And [for] some of those staff could sign up for one-on-one meetings with the consulting firm reps and kind of talk about their work at LCP and maybe some of the, shall I say, cultural challenges that they might perceive in their work.

It was all very, very loose, and it didn't feel like it was helping us move towards answering any questions about exhibitions or more successful presentations of these controversial objects, which was, I think the kind of help we were really looking for. So there had been quite a learning curve, I think, with the consulting firm and getting [them] to understand what the Library Company was already bringing to the table in terms of preparedness for this type of work and our history and commitments. And I think they started with a number of false assumptions about the staff. So we ended up just kind of parting ways with them early on and hiring Tania Isaac instead to carry on that work. But a lot of time and energy went into trying to get the work with the consultants right because we needed that kind of assistance still. And I think that was meant to be one really positive thing about "Beyond Glass Cases" for the staff was this opportunity for professional development growth.

Daniel: And so then what ended up happening with Tania?

Emily: We kind of tried to pivot and Tania did lay out a contract, if I recall, that included representing staff and project interest to the board. And also she said she was willing to talk to the board about the project and also the value of this project and kind of moving the Library Company forward and dealing with the Jennings painting and all of that stuff. And Sarah, it sounds like she didn't get to that.

Sarah: Not really. With Tania, we did have one of our regular monthly all staff meetings Tania attended, and I thought did a good job in just trying to bring the rest of the staff who were not directly working on "Beyond Glass Cases" into the project in the sense of trying to explain what it was all about, what the goals were, to say that she was available to meet with people if they'd like to talk about any concerns they had now that they understood a little bit more about "Beyond Glass Cases". So I felt like that was a good first step in carrying on what we had potentially, I guess hoped the other consulting firm would do, but Tania never had the opportunity to meet with the board.

She was scheduled, and then there was so much going on internally at the Library Company. The board was extremely distracted with other financial and personnel matters that when I was trying to get her onto the agenda, I was basically told there just isn't time. We could try to have a separate meeting that was just Tania and the board. And I said, no, actually to that because it would've wasted Tania's time, because frankly, I think the only board members who might've come were ones that really weren't the ones that needed to hear what Tania was trying to tell them and talk about. And after that, I think Tania just became very busy with her own work.

Daniel: Makes sense. Maybe it's worth also noting, without getting into the details about the behind the scenes stuff, even just sharing things that are in the public record, is that in the course of this time period, there was a leadership transition in terms of your director. There were also these conversations that have been reported on in terms of your discussions with the American Philosophical Society and about sharing resources. And so just acknowledging that those are some of the things that probably made it a complicated moment.

Sarah: Absolutely. And also to be aware that many staff members left because of what was going on, and those were not necessarily positions that were filled again. So there was a lot of internal scrambling of people trying to do other people's jobs just to keep things going. So I completely understand a certain lack of interest in "Beyond Glass Cases" or any other project. Actually, a lot of [peoples' response to what was going on] was just put your head down, just try to keep your own job, and continue to do what you know you need to do just to keep the door open.

Daniel: Well, so to shift gears a little bit, I'd like to talk about what did end up happening with "Beyond Glass Cases." So there was sort of this fumbling in some ways around the first phase, it sounds like, for various reasons. But then there was this second phase which included these experiments, these artist commissions, and I'm going to talk to the artists, but I'm wondering maybe before I get into your read on those projects, I'd love to hear a little bit more about the way that those invitations happened, the way to the artists that were ultimately selected and what the ask and the offer was to them to get engaged in this project.

Sarah: That's something probably you need to take, Emily. I really was not involved in that as it was way before the handoff.

Emily: So when the grant was written, we knew that the Jennings painting would be the center of the focus of one of the three projects. So I wrote a call for proposals for that, and I think we did a pretty good job of putting the word out. I think Erika [Piola] in the graphic arts department reached out to Mark Thomas Gibson ultimately, and just to make sure he was aware of this project. And he ended up applying, I think we got maybe six or eight applications, and the advisory committee and I think some of the staff got to make the selection. I can't remember if Erika and Linda [Kimiko August] were on the selection committee.

Sarah: Yes, I believe they were, because it was a painting, so it was in Linda's purview sort of. And then Erika as a Visual Culture Program Director, I think that they were making that selection.

Emily: Yeah, he had a really strong proposal and a strong reputation, and it seems like a really exciting opportunity for the Library Company. So that went really well. Paul Wolff Mitchell was also a presence at the Library Company when this grant was being written. I think he was finishing up a fellowship and he was making some really exciting discoveries around these Samuel George Morton manuscripts, specifically [looking at the] the draft of "Crania Americana." So I was talking to him a lot about that project, and he was very involved with activism at the Penn Museum around their use of their human remains collection. And I thought, well, this sounds like a really good fit for "Beyond Glass Cases." And he was about to get his PhD and was kind of looking for creative opportunities and different ways to use his scholarship. So he was signed up from the get-go as well.

And I think it was the original consulting firm that suggested that we leave the third project somewhat open, that we work with community, whatever that meant to them at the moment, to kind of invite them to come take a look at the library collections and work with staff to share their interests and see what we could come up with from the collections that piqued their interest. And these were all equal opportunities in terms of funding and timeline and all of that. And so we put that call out again and networked pretty well. And it turned out to be Tafari [Robertson] that was selected. Tafari had also applied for the Jennings opportunity, but his proposal seemed like, wow, this would be a really good fit for the open call. And he had some really creative ideas and seemed really ambitious, and he would be very engaged in the process. We selected him, and then each partner, Paul, Mark, and Tafari had some staff liaisons that they got to work with. So Mark got to work with Erika and Linda. Paul was working with Rachel D'Agostino and me and maybe…

Sarah: I think Wynn [Eakins] was pretty much with Tafari.

Emily: Wynn ended up being mostly with Tafari. And we did our best to just let them find their own paths and do what they wanted to do with it without putting too many constraints on it. And I will say we did not push that experimental slash prototype experience approach, but at least by at the time I left, we were doing I think a very good job of staying in communication with the participants and hearing their ideas as they were being developed and helping them figure out what, especially Tafari and Paul, how these ideas might turn into an exhibition and program.

Sarah: Yeah, I was going to say, I was going to just jump in and say, I think it was through, maybe you can correct me. Was it through Paul that we learned about We Are the Seeds? Actually, I think that was through Bill Adair. Because we also had, within the "Crania Americana" project, the musical premiere of "Project Obtuse," which was working with another creative partner that came to us through We Are the Seeds, which is a Philadelphia based organization. Zachariah Julian was the composer who was, I think he worked for, We Are the Seeds, even though he's based out of New Mexico. That's how we came to know Zach. And that was sort of part of the larger "Crania Americana" project that sort of had two equal, in my mind, equal components, the physical exhibition that was at the Library Company and the musical premiere, which was not at the Library Company.

Emily: That does remind me. Yeah. As part of Paul's process, he was rightfully reluctant to be the center of his project and be the white academic scholar who was kind of defining interpretation of the Morton collection. And we spent a long time trying to find a partner for him, a creative partner for his work. So yeah, I think it was Bill who came up with We Are the Seeds.

Daniel: Okay. And so just so I'm kind of pulling back and understanding how these unfolded. Were all these selected around the same time so that you had an idea of what would be transpiring or were these happening in a sequence in some manner?

Sarah: My recollection was all the selections were made more or less at the same time...

Emily: I think they were roughly within a couple months of each other.

Sarah: Yeah. I think the thing that could have changed was the order of when the actual projects would take place. I think that was not necessarily tied to, "well, you're the first person we selected. You're going first."

Daniel: Okay. And in terms of this, I mean feel like there's an emphasis that's made in the documentation around the project, and even in your all's re-telling that there would be these liaisons. Can you speak a little bit more to the implication of that? Obviously there's a practical, I can imagine a practical reasoning somebody needs to get into the building and get access to materials, but is there a dimension of it that also was rooted in that concept of this being impactful for the Library Company that staff would have some kind of opportunity for growth or through this process? Can you say anything about that?

Sarah: I certainly think that was part, yes, I think having the staff liaisons could be sort of a two-way street in terms of allowing the Library Company staff be part of the project who weren't necessarily written into the grant, but were nonetheless where people that had the expertise about some of the materials that our partners would be utilizing could facilitate, as you said, them getting easy access to the materials—if there was any sense of intimidation about being at the Library Company or a special collections research library could sort of smooth the way. I think it was a way for us to try to make our project partners feel welcome as well, that somebody would be their point of contact, not just whoever happened to be available when they wanted to come in or they needed something that would be a dedicated person to help them navigate and succeed.

Emily: I also just really needed their help. None of the liaisons were necessarily named in the application, nor was that strategy really discussed during the development of the project. So I really felt like I was on my own at the beginning, and I know the staff thought, what the heck is this project? How are we going to do this? Probably "poor Emily." And so kind of finding ways that they can be involved without totally taking over their time or their working lives and creating some meaningful opportunities.

Sarah: I think also being realistic with our partners, because many of us have worked with guest curators before, not necessarily part of this project, but who come in and think that they're going to, I don't know, build some amazing structure in the middle of the gallery. And it's like, okay, let's step back and ask do we have the capacity to do that, to try to not reign in their ideas and squash them in any way, but to just be realistic about what we can do and to brainstorm. Here's our project partner that wants to do this. We've never done that. Let's see if we can figure out how to make it happen or to try to modify it so we can do it. So I saw that as part of their role as well.

Daniel: Well, just continuing into these three projects, we don't have to talk about all of them, but is there something that you felt like worked particularly well just in your experience of it? And why?

Sarah: I mean, for me, I think the project that worked the best for me on a personal level was the musical performance by Zachariah Julian, which was different from anything the Library Company had done that I'm aware of. As I said, we'd worked with artists, but not with…I shouldn't say we'd never worked with musicians before, but it was so personal for him that he put a face to something that I sort of had known intellectually, but had not really absorbed personally of how damaging it was to him. And presumably to other indigenous people: the racial science [history]. His musical composition was audiovisual, it was multipronged. He involved his parents in it. They were part of a video that was going on during some of his music, and it was a very intimate take on what he saw and experienced. And I was very sad that so few people attended because I really felt like that kind of embodied what I was thinking "Beyond Glass Cases" could be. But we do have a video of the entire performance that I think we're putting on the website that hopefully that will reach more people than the forty people that attended the performance.

Emily: Well, I left before any of the projects debuted. But it was interesting to me to kind of become the outsider, the member of the public who sees what the Library Company is doing. And it was easy for me to step back and say, oh, Sarah's really seen this through in a positive way, and she helped to make all these things happen. And so I enjoyed seeing the advertisements on social media and seeing what Tafari and Mark and Paul and Zachariah did with the project. So from the outside, it looked really good, and it did look like a success, and it's nice to see that. I can't say that one seemed more successful than the others, but I was maybe especially excited to see Tafari's work, which I think perhaps was highest stakes in terms of concept and his level of experience, which was pretty minimal. And it did seem like he ran with the opportunity and built a sense of community around it. So that was good.

Sarah: I think that Mark Thomas Gibson's paintings might have been the project that resonated the most with the Library Company's kind of core constituency: the shareholders and the board. I think they were able to wrap their heads around it a little bit more of what he was attempting to do. Although I think some of them thought that his project would be more of a really direct—"here's the Jennings painting. This is what I think about the Jennings painting." And that's not what he ever said he was going to do, but I think it may have sort of morphed in some people's heads into what their expectation was. But I think the people, Library Company shareholders and the board members, people who walked through the gallery, I think were really engaged with his paintings and I think got something out of it that maybe they hadn't really understood what the rest of "Beyond Glass Cases" was about.

Daniel: So looking more critically, were there parts of "Beyond Glass Cases" that did not land within the Library Company? And as you say, Sarah, its core constituencies, its staff, etcetera. And what do you think led to that outcome and what implications might it have for how you'd do a project like this in the future?

Sarah: I found there to be an institutional lack of interest in support of the project. And some of that may be on me for not having [much social media] though Emily, apparently, liked the social media. I don't know that our traditional constituents are on social media. I think maybe many people didn't really understand what the project was. And I know from the receptions and the events that we've held, very few of our core shareholders, members, board members are attending any of them. So in that way, I feel disappointed that this was a missed opportunity, again because I think largely there was so much going on occupying at least the board's attention that they just couldn't absorb anything else that wasn't directly in their absolute wheelhouse of interest. I know the next exhibition we're doing is about, it's tying into the 250th anniversary of the founding of the Marine Corps and the Navy, and I think the curator is trying to take a slightly untraditional approach to that. But that certainly is a more traditional topic. And I think what we're doing for America 250, I think is pretty traditional as well. So I am not sure that in the long term that "Beyond Glass Cases" is going to have much of an impact at all.

Daniel: Maybe taking that as a jumping-off point, there are broader implications for this project in terms of the context that we're in, both in Philadelphia specifically and nationally more generally in terms of the upcoming 250th birthday of the country and the ways in which that celebration will be marked with critical engagement or maybe more explicitly patriotic engagement.

And so I do think that there are implications for an experiment, if you frame "Beyond Glass Cases" as an experiment, there are implications for other cultural organizations that are attempting to walk a very delicate line in terms of how they frame history in a way that is critical, but also invites people in. And so I guess I'm just also wondering about any kind of reflections you all have that might have "lessons learned" for other organizations that are trying to do this kind of work in the future.

Sarah: Have staff and board buy-in right from the start. I think what "Beyond Glass Cases" was trying and is trying to do is definitely worth doing, but as it was laid out in the grant it was so difficult to achieve that. I think if there had been more staff participation in thinking about how we could achieve what the goals were that we might have, it would've been a more rewarding process and ultimately maybe more successful because I think we could have seen some of the pitfalls that were written into the grant.

Emily: I think we're still in the moment with this project, and maybe if you had asked us this question a year from now, we'd have very different answers. But maybe because I am now on the outside, I can say that I think in many ways this is a project that maybe it's the last of its kind for a while because of the way funding is changing. And I really think one of the most important goals of the project was to not avoid, but find ways to have those generative conversations and to keep these harmful collections, that the Library Company collected for very good reasons, in the public eye and to try to do it in a way that was meaningful to people on different sides of these issues. People who might not have understood the history of race science or not had a problem with the way Penn was using human remains, but Paul and Zachariah's work allowed them to see that a little bit differently, or people who might not have understood why the staff needed to move the Jennings painting out of the reading room; maybe through Mark's work, they were able to see that a little bit differently now.

So it was hard, very, very hard and very heated for a very long time. But I hope that the project provided some, I hope that the participants had, a positive experience and that everything we were going through didn't seep out and impact them too much. I know it did on occasion, but that it was meaningful for them too, and that maybe these successes can be examples for other organizations who are wanting to try something similar and for the 250th or beyond. Yeah, absolutely.

Daniel: And so I think it's also important, while an audience may not need to get bogged down in all the specifics of what's going on in terms of staff transition there, the truth is this is what's going on in the field right now. There's a ton of turnover. There are all these organizations, all your peer organizations are in crisis. It's a challenging time. And so it's not surprising that a project that had a lot of layers to it would also run up against some of those challenges. But I think figuring out ways to share it out so that you can also be a generous member of the library and museum field and help people think through, how would we do this differently or how would we maybe adapt some of these strategies, I think could be really instructive.

Emily: Yeah, I told Sarah in a previous conversation that I think all of our original questions in the grant proposal and ideas were good ones, but had the project been designed just to be a little bit simpler, to not have quite as many moving parts would've helped a lot. It was just a whole lot to try to take on at once.

Sarah: There was also the symposium part of it too. We were able to drop that, but yes, it was just everything sort of tossed in there that was a little more than a little overwhelming.

Daniel: Well, and that's also, again, that's a layer to it, which is also about the way that funding might incentivize that kind of layered project. And so I also think it's not, you all, I can say pretty confidently, you all are not alone in being kind of overwhelmed by getting a huge project grant that doesn't quite fit into your organizational infrastructure. That's a very common kind of tension, I would say. You can't scale up internally for just such a relatively short period of time while you're still also doing your other job.

Emily: Yeah, that's what we said.

Interview: Linda Kimiko August, Rachel D'Agostino, Sharon Hildebrand, and Erika Piola

Each creative partner was paired up with at least one Library Company staff member who served as their liaison. Liaisons and partners met regularly to brainstorm ideas, review historical collection items, plan events, and to coordinate the administrative tasks necessary to bring each creative endeavor to fruition.

This interview was conducted by Daniel Tucker on June 23, 2025.

Daniel: So this is about the prehistory of "Beyond Glass Cases"—what was going on with the Library Company when this project was developing and what were conversations like five years ago? Certainly I've been witness to a long history of the Library Company doing exhibitions about progressive topics and themes that are found in your materials. But I want to get a sense of what a project like "Beyond Glass Cases" is building on.

Erika: I remember "Beyond Glass Cases" came out of a 2021 retreat of the senior staff with Bill Adair as a moderator. And there was an idea for a "collections lab," and I [recently] found the memo to staff about the collections lab with the request for us to continue that conversation. At that point, they were thinking of asking, I forget who, but they weren't going to ask the Pew Center for Arts & Heritage for money. They were going to be asking for money, I think from NEH as a starter grant. Things that I remember from that conversation and what we discussed in the memo were that these were supposed to be experiments. I remember they were supposed to be quick and cheap experiments and that we were going to get feedback. Part of the main goal of doing these experiments with difficult materials in our collections was that they would be evaluated, that these would be evaluated experiments. And I think that did continue on. That was a part of "Beyond Glass Cases," which I don't know fully came to fruition. I think that's what we're trying to do with [the] "Reflections" [exhibit as] this final part.

Linda: I guess I'd say we have worked with contemporary artists before, so that aspect wasn't new. I worked on a project that was Pew Center for Arts & Heritage-funded with an artist named Jennifer Levonian. Sarah [Weatherwax] and I worked on that, and that was for the Civil War sesquicentennial. So the topic was Civil War, but the artist could choose whatever they wanted in that. And she came and looked at lots of material and then picked a topic and made an animated film from it. So we worked with contemporary artists before. I think "Beyond Glass Cases" was the first time where we chose material. We selected the material and had the artist respond to it rather than they got to pick their own material. So that was a little different.

Erika: And Bill Adair was involved with that one too. "Common Touch" was another project that was Pew Center–funded. We worked with the artist Teresa Jaynes, and I have to say in a way that one was different from "Beyond Glass Cases" in that we had a relationship with Teresa before we started the Pew-funded project. We did another little project with her, "Moon Reader." I think it was three years before "Common Touch" was actually implemented or even our going for the money or the grant funding. And I will say something that I felt that was different between "Common Touch" and "Beyond Glass Cases." There was a group of us who were owning that project, me, Rachel, and Teresa, and you knew from the get-go who was going to be steering it, the support, the partnerships that were going to be happening. We had a plan of action, a calendar, even before the project started. And I think that was something that was missing with "Beyond Glass Cases." And I think it had affected how it was implemented, how it's been going, what our outcomes are…

Rachel: Even before "Common Touch", we worked with an artist [Jesse Lentz] a million years ago, and we also worked with the Philadelphia Cartoonist Society to do a sort of mini exhibit related to an ephemera exhibition that Erika and I curated. So there's definitely a long history, particularly connected to the Visual Culture Program of working with artists. But you also mentioned about other progressive topics in the question, and I wanted to just mention a couple. So there was "That's So Gay", which was an exhibition, and I think it was very representative of the kinds of progressive topics that we cover in the way we've covered them in the past. A lot of times we kind of skirt around it to maybe sometimes trick people into learning something that will surprise them in their progressiveness. But I think we have a long history going back to, I think it was the first exhibition when I started here, maybe twenty-five years ago or so, "Genesis of Republicanism," [which] was about the Republican Party. But the way the curator handled it, it revealed some unpleasant truths to people who might've come in thinking they were going to be like

"Rah-rah Republicans". So that's how we've handled progressive topics in the past.

Erika: I am also going to [mention the] "Hearing Voices" exhibition that Rachel and a former colleague Sophia [Dahab] were involved in. "Imperfect History" was an exhibition that Sarah [Weatherwax] and I were involved in, which was about the 50th anniversary for the graphic arts department. We got the funding in 2019/2020, in thinking about your five-year timeframe. So what was going on in 2019/2020 did influence how we thought about that project in which we were looking at the cultural and historical biases that created the collections here at the Library Company and trying to take a critical and transparent look at our own biases in what we have collected, including those who created the materials and the graphic materials that we were looking at. And I have to say that process wasn't perfect. It was also during the pandemic and later in some of the conversations we had for "Beyond Glass Cases," there were concerns raised about how we included some of that material, which has stuck with me. I'm thinking about progressive projects feeding into "Beyond Glass Cases" and "Beyond Glass Cases" is making me rethink about how those projects went. Maybe some things we might've done differently…

Sharon: So at the time they were writing the grant [for "Beyond Glass Cases"] I was interviewing for this job. And that was the entire conversation I had with the director at the time, Michael Barsanti. One of my comments to him was that I am familiar with the exhibitions that had been done here in the past, that it felt like the Library Company was already kind of doing, I don't know, cutting edge, but certainly doing a fabulous job. I felt like they were really showcasing the collection in a more current narrative and a more progressive narrative. And so it was kind of a surprise to me that they felt like something needed to be done differently. But I'm not sure in the end what came from it was as different as what had been done in the past. It feels like it continued with the same kind of standard that had already been established here.

Rachel: I just want to add one other aspect of exhibitions. When we're talking about exhibitions, we're talking about a whole package that includes the programming that goes along with them. At least that's how I'm thinking of it. It's not a standalone exhibition. So there were exhibitions that on their face might not have seemed like they were dealing with progressive topics, but then the programming would bring in some modern voices. So we have really tried for a long time to bring in other voices, artists, journalists, practitioners, things like that to try and make the collections relevant to people who don't automatically assume that they are relevant to their lives.

Linda: I wanted to mention, we've not only worked with visual artists, but also musicians. We've done a couple of Francis Johnson musical events and things, too.

Erika: And I have to say just with my hat on as the director of the Visual Culture Program, I continue to work with artists. Right now I'm working with an artist/professor at Temple University who has been bringing her classes here. She is also a part of Ortega y Gassett Projects [in Brooklyn]. There's a group of artists that she's thinking of maybe doing an exhibition here [with], and we're in the starting stages of discussion. So what I am saying is that we have a through-line of working with artists that's been happening for many years here and is continuing at the Library Company. But my working with her and my experience with "Beyond Glass Cases" has not radically altered my thinking of how I'm going to [do the work].

Rachel: If you haven't figured it out already, none of the people here were involved in the writing of the grant. But many of us thought, yes, like she said, we were already doing a lot of this stuff. And there was a painting in particular that started this conversation off. And Linda, I assume that was one of the reasons that you were involved in the earliest conversations?

Erika: Well, and at one point we were told that we were not going to go through with the grant application because the staff realized we are not ready for this. I mean, for certain aspects, dealing with DEI or having workshop groups, having focus groups—we realized we need some more tools in the tool chest before we even start, maybe a planning grant first. And so at one point there was for ten seconds like [agreement], oh yeah, that does make sense—we're not going to go through with the grant. And then let's just say our director had a discussion, with a different group of folks, and it was pushed through.

Daniel: Yeah. Well, I am hopeful in the opening essay of this publication I can also put some of the issues that have come up in a larger context. So whether it's like the way in which grant funding can drive and manipulate institutional priorities or even issues around staff turnover, and obviously that's not a unique problem to the Library Company—but that's a way in which this project seems to have been further complicated in people's experience too, is some of the passing around, whether it's leadership or in some of your cases, even other staff liaisons leaving too. So I think we'll get into all that.

So with the caveat being that not everyone was necessarily sort of evenly or appropriately consulted on this, the project seems to have been conceptualized with a couple of different dimensions to it. And those include on the one hand, working with controversial objects but also more about exhibition strategies generally, as well as working with artists, which you all have acknowledged is an ongoing practice of the organization. And so before we kind of dive in completely into the content of "Beyond Glass Cases" and your work as liaisons, I was just wondering if you could talk a little bit about those goals. Were there other goals that you saw at work in the project? Do you feel like those were all equally emphasized? How did you see them interacting in the way that the project was conceptualized and ultimately executed?

Erika: I will say one thing, for me, is that I felt like the goals were always so muddy, and I used to joke, what really are our goals? I felt like there were sort of the aspirational goals that were listed in the grant application, which I knew were not going to be the real goals that we could possibly achieve. And in all honesty too, I was like, okay, I'm supposed to be a liaison. I was not a part of the writing of the grant. Other people are supposed to be in charge of this steering in trying to implement those goals and in a way that I didn't feel it was my responsibility to implement those goals. And so I felt like I was somewhat a little removed and waiting for that guidance that I knew was never coming.

And then at a certain point for practical terms, I don't know that I ever re-envisioned or thought further about the goals. I understood this project needs to get done. We needed a calendar and to meet every month. Here are resources that we can provide, and the meetings served to get updates about our work. I mean, I will say that I think that the exhibition strategy part of the grant, that seemed to me quickly, that was out the window. Again, seeing all the [staff] who were turning over, we are not going to be updating what we're doing with exhibitions, we're not going to have a new exhibition strategy.

Rachel: Yeah, I think that's a really excellent point because I also wasn't really thinking about goals other than these are the goals set forth in the grant that are deliverables in terms of [the grant]. But in terms of sort of grander approaches to collections, things of that sort, I think that we did a great job because the people who ended up working on it were dedicated and were just the kind of people who will make things happen. But I think that this particular project suffered from the fact that the people who devised it were not in any way involved in its actual execution, and many of them were not here at all, which I kind of think we did a better job than it might have been done otherwise. I'm proud of the work we did.

Sharon: I feel like I came in late as a liaison, so I'm not sure I had a great deal of influence. I don't know if influence is the right word, but impact on that aspect. Being the person who was responsible for installation of all of the projects, I felt like my goal was to make sure the artists all saw their visions come to fruition. And I feel like with the support of each of the liaison on staff, we were able to really do that. And I feel like it was very successful for that reason: that we listened to the artistic partners that we were working with and really tried to meet their needs and meet their goals.

Linda: I feel like Michael Barsanti leaving and Emily Guthrie leaving and Rachel Hammer leaving, we had to pivot, but some of the goals that were in the original grant, we were supposed to have all the staff do training. We were supposed to go on all these field trips, and that never happened because Emily was supposed to be doing that and she left. We also had a consulting group come in that did a workshop with the whole staff and was doing more of the DEI kind of community work. And then they left and I never got an official answer as to why we stopped working with them. Then the whole DEI aspect went away to where the grant just had to get stripped down to bare bones just to bring it through the finish line. But conceptually, it was supposed to be a much more robust long-term thing where we as a staff would learn from this and take that forward. But that just didn't happen, just with all the things that were going on.

Rachel: One more comment I want to make about goals is I kind of set it as my own personal goal, though. I think it definitely built into the role of the liaison to protect our partners and both sort of shielding them from the chaos that might've been going on behind the scenes, but also trying to prepare the artist in particular for the emotional impact of what he was about to see and work with. And I think that's a really important goal for a liaison. And I felt as though I couldn't do that to the best of my abilities because of the background chaos that was happening.

Daniel: Well, let's use that as an occasion to jump into talking more about the liaison roles. But as a sort of a sidebar, just because you brought it up, Rachel, I mean, I have interviewed all the creative partners already, and I will say I feel like they reflected that they felt cared for by you all. So for what it's worth…

Rachel: That's good to hear. Thank you for sharing.

Daniel: So in terms of your roles as liaisons, could you maybe each go through and talk about the specific project that you worked with and what it looked like? I guess practically, but also emotionally, politically, and creatively to interface with these creative projects.

Sharon: Well, the first project was the "Black Historians' Department." And that is the project that I came in on to work with Tafari Robertson. Tafari had been working with Wynn Eakins, who did a fabulous job of introducing Tafari to a lot of items in the collection. He didn't select a particular object, but it was more focused on his experience and maybe interpretation of what it was like as a Black researcher going into primarily white or historically white institutions to look at collections. And I hope he had a different experience at the Library Company, but his project was informed by experiences that he and his colleagues had previously. He spent a lot of time interviewing friends and other scholars who shared their experiences and those experiences weren't always positive. The concept of setting up this "Black Historians' Department" where the history and knowledge could be shared in ways that reflected their background and experiences was an important component to the exhibition.

    So a lot of the work that had been done had already happened by the time I started working with Tafari. And so I tried to take the situation where he was at the time, and then as he needed to pivot, I would pivot with him to try to give him the installation that he visualized the "Black Historians' Department" being. And it was kind of invigorating for me. I really enjoyed it, having always worked on the other side of exhibitions. I worked at the PMA [Philadelphia Museum of Art] for fourteen years, so I worked with curators and with artists, but in that role it was how do you want this framed or how do you want this exhibited and not actually being able to do that intellectual work with an artist or a scholar. So I really enjoyed this and feel like it fed me maybe more than I was able to feed anything into the project, but that was my experience.

Daniel: Yeah, that's great to hear. Thanks Sharon.

Rachel: I worked on "Project Obtuse/Crania Americana," and each of these projects has a different origin story. And this one was peculiar in that we were working with a scholar who had been researching in the collection of the Samuel George Morton papers. So that scholar's name is Paul Wolf Mitchell. He's now based in the Netherlands, and he had been discovering some really amazing things in the Morton Papers. When I was brought in to this project, it had already been written into the grant, if I recall correctly, that one of the projects would be involving Paul and this collection of papers. So it took me a little while to figure out what the project was actually going to focus on because Paul was making these incredible discoveries, but that was not what the project was going to focus on. That was sort of secondary and that's something Paul still is working on.

So I started working with Paul, and Paul has many, many connections all over the country, all over the world, really, of people working in the history of scientific racism and particularly in collections related to this book that was developed by Morton. So Paul and I were having regular meetings and we were reaching out to people to interview to just get a sense of how they felt about a project that would focus on this material and is there an artist they could recommend. We were put in touch by one of those scholars with We Are the Seeds, a Philadelphia-based organization that focuses on indigenous artists and the current life, contemporary life of indigenous Americans. They're Philadelphia-based. We got incredibly fortunate, I think by being directed to them, who then directed us to Zachariah Julian, and Zachariah is based in New Mexico. So our work, the three of us together, was done remotely. We met very frequently; Zach was able to make a couple of research trips up here. So we spent a little more time together that way. But it was different from the other projects in that it had this scholar and an artist and that we were all so geographically dispersed all around. I think we got so lucky finding Zachariah and convincing him to work with us.

Linda: So myself, Erika, and Wynn Eakins were working with Mark Thomas Gibson. I should say that I went on disability at the end of May, so I was there for Mark and his assistant, Alex, who would come regularly, look at the painting, and also look at other related material in our graphics collection related to figures of liberty and things like that. I thought those meetings went really well. And then we set up listening sessions. I thought Wynn did a great job of connecting us with some groups. That was really hard. You really need someone who's plugged into a group. It's very hard to just cold-call or cold-email a group and ask them to volunteer their time and come in to talk about something that's difficult. So I thought the listening sessions went very well, and Mark started doing sketches and things, and then I went on disability. So Erika carried it through after that point.

Erika: I think Wynn left around May too. So it was May or June. Yeah. So yeah, it was me, Wynn, and Linda as liaisons until May 2024, and Mark's exhibition went up in October 2024. So the last few months it was me carrying the mantle, but at that point, a lot of Mark's conceptualizations had already been done. He had done the research and we were heading into the part of getting the kind of nuts and bolts of the exhibition together. And for Mark's exhibition—he did four paintings that were inspired by "Liberty Displaying the Arts and Sciences" and his reading of that painting, and its looking toward the future. So then the listening sessions were based on questions to folks to think about the future of Philadelphia [and] the country.

And Mark was very cognizant through this process too—that his paintings were going to be up after the election and that the election was going to be an influence on them as well. And it was an influence in the listening sessions—a lot of times that did come up. There was also a listening session with Library Company staff, which didn't become an official painting, but I think it was also a part of the conversations that were influencing what Mark was thinking about and did also affect his work. I'll say for my part that when I started to feel a bit down on the work; every time I had a conversation with Mark, it totally uplifted me. I found him so inspirational. I think certainly what Sharon was saying about feeling fed; those conversations and just how dedicated he was did keep me going.

Also, Mark was an artist who is involved in 50 billion things at the same time, but when he was with us, he seemed focused on what he was doing for us and those conversations and what he was thinking about for the project. And I so appreciated that. And I think it was also, we were fortunate that he had an assistant that I think also helped with organizing this part of the "Beyond Glass Cases." I think if we were just dealing with Mark directly, we might not have his schedule and a calendar. We were very mindful in terms of programming. We would need to program things pretty far in advance. His schedule was so chaotic; we were very appreciative of that.

Even though we'd worked with artists before, I think Mark's exhibition very much transformed the space into the most feeling like an artist's gallery, which I think really helped in the close engagement with his works and just the feedback, especially after the exhibition, people coming in and really having an emotional experience with that work…[Even in the hotline audio] someone was like, I needed this. I needed to see this.

Daniel: We'll have an opportunity to reflect on both the implications for the field and the Library Company. But in terms of just the experiences that you had with these projects, either the public-facing results or maybe the more private time in the archives, was there anything about these interventions that happened that you felt like was a real special contribution of these projects to the Library Company? They don't have to be material. They could also be just conceptual or more emotional.

Rachel: I think what really has stuck with me is how much people are really affected by what they're seeing in the collections. I mean, we knew that it was part of what stirred a lot of these conversations. For example, the issue surrounding [the "Liberty" painting] hanging in the reading room, people were coming in and saying that they were having a negative experience in that space because of that work of art being positioned as it was without context. And I think most of us on staff took those concerns seriously, very seriously. But even so, I found myself feeling distressed and a bit helpless when I would see Zachariah working in the collection and coming across something that wasn't related directly to the Morton Papers, but was related to his own history and the history of indigenous Americans. And he came to read something in the newspaper. He was curious to see what was in the newspaper. I don't think he expected what he found, which was disturbing to him. And so really this whole project, and I know because of the relationship he and I built, I know how deeply that impacted him and for how long.

So I think what will stay with me forever is a real deep understanding of how significant an impact viewing these collections can have on people. And at the same time, we see that it can have a very negative impact on someone who feels pain from what they're seeing. I think it really put into relief, how significant it can be to interact with our collections, whether they're hurtful or they're uplifting or whatever it is. It really, it was that having that person in the reading room looking at those collections and physically interacting with them, that I strongly believe it wouldn't have had that same emotional impact digitally, nor would we as curators have had the opportunity to see what impact it was having, if that makes sense.

Erika: I think something else that was sort of interesting for me with Mark's works was—and let's just say—our director's not a very visual person. But he was very taken by Mark's paintings, which I think does say something. And the night of the opening there was this really kind of, I'm using the term, lovely—that's maybe not quite the right word—moment where Mark had a case of our original materials on display that was in our reception room off of our front desk. And at one point he was looking at our digital catalog for images, and one of the materials that he wanted wound up being our Minerva sculpture in our director's [office], which is huge. And it's like there's no way, I mean, it's huge. So that became sort of funny. Yeah, we could do a reproduction, but we can't get the original. And we're like, do you want to see this sculpture in person? And so we took him and his assistant and the gentleman who hung the paintings into John [Van Horne's] office, and they had this quick conversation about the sculpture. And I think John probably interacted more so with him than any artist we've ever had working with our materials than ever before. And it was a really nice discussion. I think it just helped with the feeling, the really good feeling for that opening. So I appreciated that moment.

Rachel: The project that I worked with, there was an exhibition. It was a small exhibition in the usual space, but the performance itself was offsite. Our director did not attend the performance. I don't know that there were any board members or liaison members that went to the exhibition. Most staff did not attend the performance. And that was a real shame, I think, because that was the whole meat of the thing. And we showed a video of the performance later to staff who were interested and everyone was impacted by it. But that was a real disappointment to me and to see in particular the lack of support and interest among our administration and board. That was disappointing.

Sharon: Thanks for bringing it up, Rachel, with you on that.

Daniel: So in terms of a more critical perspective, and certainly you all have kind of hinted at these already, what would you say are parts of the project that just didn't land within the organization? Do you think that there was something in particular that led to that outcome? And just what implications does it have for the Library Company doing this kind of work more generally?

Erika: I think this plays into what Rachel was saying about the support of the administration or staff or the board. I think that there wasn't that kind of buy-in or support. And I think that was part of feeling outside of the writing process of the grant. I think it might be also that we have two big grants going at the same time. Typically in the past we'd have one big one where most of the staff was involved in some way, probably the staff turnover didn't help. Morale has been down for various reasons here at the library. I've been here almost twenty-eight years. This is a very low time at the Library Company for various reasons.

And I think in terms of what I mentioned with Mark—the opening was wonderful, really good feelings. But then there was a little bit of a, it was a roller coaster, let's say. What happened is that Mark had a conversation with a board member that made him feel like he had been taken advantage of in a way that was never meant. And I felt, as Rachel was saying, we never wanted the artist to feel harmed in this process. And I felt after that the artist felt harmed, and that made me feel horrible. And I know it's not about me, it shouldn't be about me. And I also was realizing as part of, especially with projects like this, you don't know what else is going on in folks' lives that affects how they are handling the work or handling this kind of experience or engagement with harmful materials, using these materials for a generative purpose. Mark often said it was his goal to have it be a generative project. So yes, that was another low point. And something obviously that did not land well.

We did have another opportunity to talk with Mark. Mark met with us and I think things were smoothed over, but there was a discussion for us to do another program, which did not happen because basically in all candor, he said, "I want nothing more to do with this." After he had that conversation with the board member. But again, we had that follow-up conversation, which I think did smooth things over. We saw Mark at the final "Beyond Glass Cases" "Reflections" exhibition opening. I had a lovely talk with him, we were good. It was good. And I really so appreciated him taking the time to talk with me. And we talked politics, I have to say. And he seemed really good. I think he has now decided to take a little bit of downtime. I mean, instead of sixty projects, he was going to do thirty. And I have to think maybe that's also partly his work with "Beyond Glass Cases" kind of led him to that in a good way. Not in a bad way. For me, thinking something that didn't land was feeling like an artist got harmed in this process, which is not what any of us wanted.

Sharon: I think that kind of takes us back to what Linda was saying earlier too, about all of the staff development projects or programs that were supposed to be a part of this project that didn't happen. I don't know that we could have been any more prepared than we were, but it didn't feel like we always had the tools or institutional support we needed to carry out these projects.

Rachel: And particularly once the administration switched from Mike to John as Director, to me felt like a step backward in terms of the institution having progressive values or goals. I feel like the staff who worked on these projects, all of us here and others as well, were impacted by these projects and did learn a lot from them. And I felt mine at least was a life-changing experience. But I lament that I don't see the impact of our projects on the institution as a whole. And I, of course, in our current status of we don't know what our future holds, it feels a little sad to me that at least we got something out of it, at least our artists did. But it doesn't feel like the institution grew because of this project.

Linda: I feel like community-building is really difficult and ongoing work. You really need to be committed and have the intention. And I feel like the Library Company doesn't have the institutional support or the staff support to continue ties with the community. We tend to reach out to a community, and I feel strongly that we look for a community that is going to be appealing to grant funders. We ask that community to do really hard, difficult emotional labor, and then it's a one-off project and we never connect with that community ever again. And it's just exploiting. That's how I feel.

Sharon: Yeah, I agree. Linda, when I first was brought onto the project, my biggest concern that I expressed was that it not be performative. And I feel like as an institution, not necessarily for those of us who worked with the artists, but for the institution, it was just like we're crossing this off our list now and we're done. And we didn't build those communities or make that ongoing commitment…

Erika: I'm sorry, Sharon. And that was even a concern with "Common Touch," reaching out to individuals who are blind. And I remember during that project talking to one of our liaisons, and expressing that sentiment. It was good, because they responded—it's okay—you're doing it now. You're doing the best that you can. And I mean, I do feel like there were little changes that came from that, things we do with our exhibitions. I mean, one of the big ones is the fonts we use with our labels changed. Something changed a little bit with the way we do our website. So I take that with me. But part of it, and this is probably me also rationalizing a bit, is that you don't continue to have that funding or get a staff member who is dedicated in community engagement, it's hard to continue that work. You're going onto your next grant project or the next institutional priority and you can't dedicate your time to further the previous project. And as Linda said, there is emotional labor to that work.

Daniel Tucker: Well, I think that this addresses one of my follow-up questions that was really about larger lessons for the field because you all are, I think, reflecting a lot of things that have particularity to the Library Company but are also just these ethical questions which are being felt across the sector. So I'll come back to that, but I did have one other follow-up question that is more of a clarifying question.

Something that I haven't really gotten clarity on with this project is the way, in the implication of it being kind of an artist-driven process, and for you all, in what ways is that a useful process to give over content control to an artist versus a kind of process where you might be working with an artist, but still really having a heavier curatorial hand where you're shaping the message and it not being entirely driven by the artist's interpretation? I'm just wondering for you all as liaisons, how you kind of thought about that balance and any implications that it had and if you have thoughts about doing it differently in the future?

Sharon: I feel like for Tafari and the "Black Historians' Department," not giving him full license would've been a very different message. I feel like we all maybe felt a little bruised by some of his conclusions that institutions don't treat Black scholars well. I feel like we all believe and we all certainly try to the best of our ability to do better. And so his conclusions didn't feel like they maybe rang true for us, but it wasn't about us. And so if we'd had more of a creative license over the message that was being sent, it would've been very different, I think. Which is why I think it's important that he had that opportunity to share his experiences and perspective. And you accept it and realize that, yeah, this is the reality and we don't have that experience. That's not the experience that we as white people have.

Rachel: Working with a musician who's creating a performance piece, at least the way it actually played out, was that I had no idea what I was about to see. I was almost as clueless as everyone in the audience on that night of the performance, and that was how I wanted it. But that's a huge risk. So I certainly feel that as much latitude as possible, that endless latitude should be given to artists, that it's ridiculous to invite them in and then control what they do. Erika and I worked on "Common Touch", and I was particularly working with the artist as she was [bringing] things together, and there was a part of the exhibition that wasn't installed until during the actual opening. So in terms of managing artists, I think it's important to have deadlines clearly communicated and all of that. But beyond that, I think it's really, really vital to give them total creative control. And sometimes it's hard because we feel like what criticisms they give might be aimed at us personally when they're actually meant for the institution.

And all we can control are ourselves. The four of us on this call that are staff, we can't control the institution at large. Unfortunately, that's become blindingly clear.

Erika: I will say I think it was also very helpful that we had regular meetings with Mark; we met every month as he was going through his process, and he would update us on what he was thinking. And I think that gave us opportunities to ask questions or address concerns. And he was always open from the beginning if we did have questions and concerns to address them, talk to us about them. And I can't remember all the specifics, but there was one thing when he was thinking about the work, he said something about his understanding of the artists, that is what Jennings was thinking. And I remember Wynn had some questions about that and he was open to talking with them about it.

And I don't think, again, we are not trying to steer as Sharon and Rachel are saying, I think when we were in this project, we were like, it was artist-driven. We were not going to say, oh, oh, no, no, we really want this to be in blue. And we may think that, but we were never going to do anything like that. And so far things have worked out.

But I remember once I had a conversation with another former director, and I forget which project it was on, but it was about an artist using our materials to create a work. And he's like, well, what if they create a work with the middle finger? Are we going to be open to that and putting that on our wall? And so you take some time to pause, but I guess I'd respond, "well, you're the Director. We've agreed to doing this, that we are leaving ourselves open. Yes, that's a possibility. And we'll have to walk through that door together, so to speak."

Rachel: I'm just going to piggyback on that real quick. None of us, as far as I know, received any training on how to be a liaison for a project like this. We're all long out of school, so if it had been covered in school, but none of us, I certainly was never told this is how you liaise on behalf of a cultural institution with an artist, no training whatsoever.

Erika: But I think it did help. I mean, all of us have now had experiences with liaising with artists, and Sharon, through your work, through PMA, Yes. I think we've not had the training, but we've had enough, I think, practical experience. I still feel like there's tools I can use in a tool chest at this point, but I understand. Yeah, I know what you're saying, Rachel.

Rachel: If it weren't the four of us who had liaised and it were four other employees who had a different concept of their role in relation to the artists, things could have been very, very different.

Daniel: Yeah, I mean that's part of why I asked the question is both in terms of the specificity of the institution, there's a way in which some of the work you all were doing was kind of curatorial. Some of it was project management; it was a kind of hybrid role. Some of it was research support, and of course many other things that don't have those formal titles. And so sometimes it's a question of who does what kind of work and what the implications of that is. And as you note too about not having training, what that training would look like has a lot of different versions. There's one version that centers more community engagement, whereas there's another kind of training that might be more about artist relations in a way. And so it's useful to name this. I think just in terms of lessons for the field, if anyone has any other kind of thoughts about like, oh, this is what I would tell a similar institution thinking about how to work with artists to present kind of an explore controversial objects within the collection, would be happy to hear any of that from you all.

Rachel: I think a lot of our project was handled in chaos, and I think we did a tremendous job. I think under another circumstance, it would be helpful for there to be more communication between administration and the boots on the ground as it were. But in our situation, I was glad not to have that because we were able to do our own thing. But things could have gone poorly, particularly with the change in administration. So having just real clarity on whose roles are whose, what is the actual goal of this, what will success look like agreed upon by the individuals involved and in the administration would I think be a more successful project.

Interview: Bill Adair and Tania Isaac Hyman

A six-member advisory committee was formed during the planning stage of "Beyond Glass Cases". Composed of leaders in the arts, educational, and cultural community, members offered support in their areas of expertise throughout the-three-year project. Bill Adair served as committee chair and Tania Isaac Hyman also engaged with the Library Company as a consultant.

This interview was conducted by Daniel Tucker on March 24, 2025.

Daniel: Just before we get started with my questions for you, my impression is that there are many lessons to be learned from this process and that at least in my conversations with Sarah [Weatherwax], she doesn't seem to have any reservations about sharing those lessons. And so I am inclined to create a publication that will actually be useful to the field while documenting the project itself. Hopefully useful in terms of other organizations attempting to critically engage with history generally or their own histories specifically. And I think that that's also going to be something that, as you all are well aware, will be very fraught in the next few years.

Bill: Yeah, it's kind of interesting, a context that I think you're probably be-coming aware of is that although institutional critique has been a thing at art museums for a couple of decades, it hasn't really necessarily, it hasn't been the same in history institutions. I mean, there hasn't been a kind of an institutional critique movement, let's put it that way, in the same way anyway. But ironically, I think history institutions have actually changed more than art institutions also at the same time. That's my read on the sit-uation, and I think this is an example of a very conservative organization, not necessarily in their collecting policies, but in everything else being willing to really consider working in a totally different way.

Daniel: Your point about institutional critique I think is sort of a good lead into this Bill. I want to talk a little bit about prehistory and for you all, I think in some ways the prehistory may also reach into your own practices. What kinds of things were you up to in advance of your engagement with the Library Company?

I also want to keep it somewhat focused on your read of the Library Company as an organization prior to them embarking on this process. And so I'd love just to know a little bit about what you understood the Library Company to be doing before "Beyond Glass Cases?" Even in my awareness, they've done exhibitions on progressive themes and topics before, but maybe they didn't do it in this exact same way. And so just want to know what you think that this project is building on.

Tania: I was going to say, I'll let you [Bill] start since you have a longer institutional history than I do, but maybe the reverse makes sense. So I would say I was aware, more peripherally aware of the Library Company as a historical resource. It was not a place that I went to regularly, and I was not connected to it as part of my artistic practice, research practice necessarily. I hadn't attended events there. I had looked at their information online at different points in time, and so Bill brought me into the project as part of the artist advisory committee. And so I became familiar with the goals of the project then.

And then as we continued meeting and there was a departure with their initial consulting firm. [So] we discussed having me take on that role with them, and at the time, I was really interested in institutional practice as a creative process and a creative practice itself—in terms of what questions we're asking, how we're looking at communication, how we're sort of improvising and problem-solving around something that was as true to its intent as possible. And so that's the way that I entered more conversation with them and began the interaction with staff. I was asking a lot of questions about where people had landed in terms of their relationship to the project and had a series of interviews, conversations, and some recommendations for them based on that set of interactions.

Daniel: I think we'll get more into some of that process, Tania, but I'm wondering just before Bill picks it up, I want to follow up on something we were talking about in terms of the intersection of creative and institutional processes and just see if you could share a little bit about maybe there was a project or an engagement that you had in the past that led you to examine and be invested in that intersection?

Tania: Yeah, I would say that it was my university experience. I taught for five years at Drexel University, and…it's a relatively small program, so there's a heavy lift of administration in addition to the teaching practice itself, and I became curious just about institutional function in the sphere of art-making because there are all of these conversations and all of these parameters and guidelines that we set up in the studio about how we interact, how we give feedback, our regard, our values. And taking that and moving it into the administrative work that we had to do, the interactions changed a lot. And I imagine, I would say, I imagine based on the necessity of communicating with the business part of the institution. But I think I was really intrigued by the fracture between how we created work and how we interacted as an artistic community and how we sort of morphed and shifted when we needed to do the administrative institutional work and wondering whether there was a way to bring more of those kinds of interactions and conversations together.

So I actually left Drexel in 2017, I believe, and went to Penn to the Fels Institute of Government, to do a master's in public administration and focused on policy, but also was taking courses in organizational dynamics, and had some really fascinating conversations around business practices that were starting to use the language of artistic process. They talked about improvisation, they talked about choreography, they talked about staging, and it was sort of just the bare outline of what those practices actually entailed. And to me, and I'm going to go off on my little soapbox tangent for a little bit, to me seemed more coercive than the suggestion of the integrity that was initially part of the artistic process. And so as in graduating, I was trying to figure out how to be part of institutional conversations that could actually explore those values in more holistic ways.

Daniel: That's super interesting Tania. Bill, can you share your read on the Library Company and how it intersected with things you were involved with historically?.

Bill: But I mean, the work that I've been doing my whole career is influencing as Tania's saying, well, she hasn't really said it yet, but I know it is influencing the work that we're doing at ArtPhilly. So that's another conversation. But we've both been able to experiment with putting our theory into practice with this new organization that we started from scratch.

I have known the Library Company, yes, my whole career, and I always viewed it as one of the most open of the research libraries in terms of collections policy. My knowledge of their collections policy, which I think is relatively correct, is that they began actively and intentionally collecting materials related to the history of people of color in the sixties before there was that intention in almost any other place in Philly. And the same for the history of women. And there've been these moments over the years. They did this awesome project called "That's So Gay". I don't remember if Pew funded it or not, honestly, but I was very aware of it when it was happening. They had Spiral Q do a project, Eli Nixon did a project; they did a project about who decides what's in an archive. So anyway, big picture wise, I always thought the Library Company, I've always perceived the Library

Company as really groovy. And I had good relationships with the librarians there, who always did really, to me, always seemed like they were in the forefront of collecting policies.

My own work at the Rosenbach Museum and Library, which in some ways is similar in terms as an institution where I brought artists into work there, contemporary artists to work there. And I did that in order to bring new perspectives on collections that generally were not really activated. They tend to be just, they were books and pieces of paper and tough for the public to interact with. And so one of my strategies when I was director of education at the Rosenbach was to utilize artists and their talents to activate collections that were often perceived as very impenetrable.

And I did that for, I was there for ten years and worked with a number of artists. And yeah, I saw people's perceptions of work change. As a result, I saw audiences become much more engaged with the poetry of Marianne Moore. who the freak cares about the poetry of Marianne Moore anymore. And her stuff is actually amazing, and it was because Sebastian Mannheim did an amazing thing about her. And anyway, I don't need to sort of brag about my stuff at the Rosenbach. There's a chapter called in the book "Letting Go? Sharing Historical Authority in a User-Generated World" called "The Fever Dream of the Amateur Historian: Ben Katchor's The Rosenbach Company: a Tragicomedy" by Melissa Rachleff. That is about the rock opera we did there, and it's very rocky life at the Rosenbach. I was almost fired because of that thing. I had to publicly apologize to the board, because it offended some board members. Anyway, that's to say that I have found working with artists in these kinds of institutions, very effective in audience engagement and very risky in terms of the institution's appreciation of it and willing to absorb it as a way of working.

Daniel: I hope we can revisit that in terms of ways that this project does get incorporated back into the institution, which I think you both can speak to. So you all were both involved in the external advisory committee, and obviously you work together now at ArtPhilly, so there's various reasons to talk to you as a pair, but you also played different roles as external consultants, and so you had these multiple hats, multiple vantage points, and wondering if you can describe those roles as deeply as makes sense, but also maybe ground it in some pivotal conversations that you felt like you had that gives us a sense of the stakes of the project in a way?

Bill: Yeah, I can start, I guess since my involvement in the project was earlier. So Mike Barsanti [the former Director of The Library Company] asked me to lead a brainstorming retreat for Library Company senior staff. I don't remember when, a long time ago, six years ago, seven years ago, it first, it was when I first started doing my consulting. I had left Pew [Center for Arts & Heritage] by then. So it was early on anyway, with the purpose being to consider new methods of, I don't even know if that's the right way to put it, with the purpose of considering if the exhibitions program that they had was the best way for them to present their materials to the public, asking questions about that. And in the course of that brainstorming session, this idea emerged of inviting artists to address some of the objects, the collections that were the most kind of complicated to talk about and difficult to present in sensitive, thoughtful ways.

So as a result of that kind of brainstorming retreat, this idea emerged and then became a Pew application, which was funded. The application was drafted by Mike and The Library Company's director of development at the time, Raechel Hammer. Which happens frequently, it was put together without a ton of discussion with other staff members because it had to be done quickly. And I really don't want to throw Mike or Raechel under the bus here, frankly, because I think their intentions were really, really good. They wanted to try something new, and they just went ahead and did it. They just went ahead and wrote this thing without talking to a lot of people. And I think some of that was just expediency. I don't think there was any nefarious intentions or anything like that, of course, anyway. But what happened is that it got funded and then suddenly this project had to be done, and they brought in the staff at that point to get buy-in on the project when it had already been conceived and funded. And that, in and of itself, I think was problematic and threw a giant wrench in the institution's relationship to the project from the beginning.

Daniel: I'll just say, I just interviewed Sarah Weatherwax and Emily Guthrie and they said the same thing, but it does bring up some larger issues in terms of the way in which, as you say, you don't have to throw anybody under the bus, but it's more of a question of the ways in which funding does incentivize organizations to sometimes overreach.

Bill: Great point. Yeah, exactly. In some ways, I think that this project was designed to get a Pew grant, and yes, I think that that is part of the story here, when the organization itself might not have been ready for this particular kind of project, but it was designed to match what Pew would fund.

And then once the project was funded, Mike asked if I would be the chair of the advisory committee and work with Emily on the project because I had been there kind of right from the start. And that's the history of, I mean, that's how I got involved.

Daniel: Okay, great. Tania?

Tania: So in the conversations with the advisory board when things were not moving forward with the original consulting firm, I met with Bill and Emily and we talked about the potential for the kind of work that I had started doing to move into that role with the Library Company. And it seemed like a really good fit. And I submitted a proposal that included speaking with the staff, potentially speaking with the board, sort of looking at where the project was and what could bring the threads together more thoughtfully, what could create a more sort of multidimensional approach to the kind of engagement that they wanted to do that they weren't quite seeing.

And so it started out with, I met with as much of the staff as could be present, and we just talked; actually, we didn't talk at first. I had them write out their concerns about the aspirations for the project, which I gathered, and then sort of created a summary that we used for the next set of meetings. And what came to bear, as you both have talked about, is the anxiety of the staff in not quite understanding, not just the overall goals of the project, but also all of the administrative mechanisms that would make it possible to have these artists come in to create things on a timeline that made sense to be engaged with the appropriate audiences in ways that did not feel extractive. All of those considerations had not yet been made, and were trying to do it on the fly. And so, so I created with them sort of series of questions that they could ask internally, and then some questions that they could pose to both the artists and to the external partnerships that they had in terms of gauging what the possibilities were for the relationship and the idea also of being realistic given the origins of the project, given the time constraints of looking at what might not necessarily be a huge institutional shift, but a really clear focused engagement with the artists around the goals of their particular project.

So for example, we were [asking] them:

Within the project goals, are we able to distill what we agree that we're trying to accomplish and why? How do we ensure that the events communicate what the artists want? What are the sticking points and why? In less-than-ideal circumstances, what can we create? What remains important and achievable? And a lot of questions of that nature. But what really became clear was there was just not enough time left in the project to pursue it in the way that everybody would've preferred. And what I saw was a lot of investment in the staff that I spoke to in bringing the project forward as well as the hesitation about what kind of institutional impact it could have, because there was not that sort of structure for support, but there was also not a lot of great communication with the board about how these things would unfold and not a lot of support in terms of their presence that [would give] it some more validity, I guess.

Daniel: Well, thanks for reading those out. I was curious to hear that, and it's helpful to hear a little bit about the process. I also want to kind of pull back and say, so there was this advisory committee. Is there anything to say about that body, did that body assemble, did it have input on artists selections? What happened there? What was the advisory committee? How was it used?

Tania: So we met with Emily pretty regularly, especially at the beginning of the project in terms of writing the "Call for artists" in looking at the proposals that came in and making our own recommendations and taking those to the staff, and it was really a joint [effort]. We did not select on our own the artists, that was in collaboration with the staff and everyone at the Library Company taking into account our recommendations and making the final decisions themselves, and then conversations about some potential directions for the project itself and what kinds of activities could happen. Some of the challenges in the transfer, like we were talking about coming from one leader through the other, trying to integrate it into what was happening with other things at the time.

Bill: I think before Tania started, we'd had a few meetings. So Emily put together the advisory committee of people that she knew had been working basically in their whole careers on trying to expand audiences for these kinds of collections, expand and diversify the audiences for these kinds of collections and people that she knew and could trust. Because Emily was suddenly put in charge of this project that she was like, eh, she didn't, didn't write the application to Pew, and she was made project director.

Anyway, so Mike and Raechel had put this consulting group into the application, which was a west coast consulting firm whose job it was to help guide us through conversations about diversity and equity and race. And a representative from the consulting firm came to one of our first meetings with the advisory committee. And so this is going to be a Roshomon thing, but I have my perspective on that and my perspective on it is that she did not know her audience at all. She hadn't done homework about who we were, and it was like a race training, a diversity training 101 for a corporation that had never ever thought about race and diversity in its existence.

It was the wrong tone and the wrong message to the audience that she was talking to. She would say things like, "there are stories to be told that are not just white stories" and stuff like that to people that had been working their whole careers on, you know what I mean?

And it was very alienating at first. It just kind of felt like a waste of time. And then it became alienating because, and I think Emily and I kept trying to send her the message that, well, the Library Company's actually been collecting stuff from people of color for fifty years now, so not, it's not like we're starting from scratch here. And she read that as defensiveness, and perhaps it was at least somewhat, but I kept trying to just encourage her to understand, to try and meet us where we were, which is very open to learning and discussing things. But we weren't in kindergarten with this stuff and…this is my memory of the conversation, was that she got really kind of angry because she felt like we were just pushing back on listening to any kind of diversity critique.

Then we got off of that meeting and Emily called the guy who runs the consulting firm and said something like, "we don't want her to come back." This is my version, my version. And he had the same reaction as she did, which is like, oh, well, "you just don't want to hear it. You just don't want to actually critique yourselves." And Emily and I were frustrated about that, and Emily asked me to have a conversation just with the two of us, me and the head of the consulting firm. And I had a conversation with him in which I said, I used the word dramatic, overly dramatic. In describing the consultant's reaction to our conversation at the advisory committee meeting, I said that we were trying to communicate something to her, and she had a very overly dramatic reaction. She got kind of angry, and then he became very offended because I had described a woman of color as overly dramatic and was like, he was pretty pissed. It wasn't the right language for me to use. I think I immediately changed it. I think I said overly dramatic, and then I changed…I said, not really overly dramatic, but I don't even remember. Anyway, but I said it, he was pissed and he was ready to go for me. So then we got off the phone, I think we calmed down or he calmed down, whatever. I wasn't really upset about any of it. And then he called Emily and said to Emily that I should apologize to him. So then I, I think I had to apologize at an advisory committee meeting. I had to apologize for being insensitive at an advisory committee meeting and whatever. I've apologized so many times in my career for so many things, many that it didn't really bother me at all, but it really pissed Emily off. She felt like I

was very mistreated. And so right from the beginning, the advisory committee was this fraught thing.

Daniel: Well, I'll stop you all there. I want to get into the project, but I will
just editorialize slightly in case it offers sort of invitations for other things
for you to share as we move forward. Things like that happen all the time,
right, Bill, and of course there's a lot to say about it, not even in terms of the
specifics, but in terms of it's sort of the larger cultural and political moment.
Obviously we're in a moment of backlash against DEI and disciplining of
that practice broadly, which doesn't always allow for there to be a more
nuanced conversation about what does and doesn't work about trainings,
say in different contexts. And because that's not the priority right now to
have a nuanced conversation about that at the same moment as there's this
sort of severe attack going on. But it is an interesting thing to explore in
terms of lessons learned for other peer organizations.

Bill: No question.

Daniel: How do you know your audience? How do you invite trainers in to
do the right work you need them to do?

Bill: Right. Yeah, yeah, exactly. That was part of the, I feel like the consulting
firm was not the right organization, and that was the problem right from the
beginning. I think Mike just Googled consulting firm for museum diversity.
And he found them and there was no real discussion. They didn't know
what they were getting into and vice versa.

Daniel: And if so he made the same mistake a lot of executive directors have
made in not being rigorous enough about that solicitation and selection
process. So yeah, it's unfortunate. So I want to dig into, use this as a
jumping-off point to talk about "Beyond Glass Cases" and the multidimensional goals that I see at work in the project, which include how to
deal with controversial objects in their collection, how to work with artists
to interpret that collection, and then also the other dimension, which is
experimenting with exhibition strategies and public engagement strategies.
Can you all say a little bit about how you saw those goals interacting,
how you saw them being articulated within the project? Were there other
goals that I'm missing that felt kind of important in the conversations
you were having?

Tania: I think one thing that came up as a concern, I don't think I heard you
mention, was in terms of shifting perception of the Library Company as an
organization and having broader public connection, bringing more people
in for a range of reasons.

Bill: There was a fundamental question always at play, which was that should they even try? Should the Library Company even have a public exhibition program? Yeah.

Daniel: I mean, obviously in terms of actually doing this project, they were attempting to reinvigorate their public programs and exhibitions. So do you think that, when you say that that was a question, was that a question that was somehow kind of beneath the surface of the project, or was it something that was kind of happening on the side, or do you feel like it was actually centered in the work that they wanted to answer that question?

Bill: I think there was a flaw in the experiment in that there were two hypotheses that were basically the organization needed to consider, and they were both mixed up. Two questions, I guess rather than hypothesis: should there be an exhibitions program at all at the Library Company to serve the public? And the other being, how do we exhibit and talk about controversial/difficult objects? And those two questions got mixed up, and it was one of the problems with the project from the beginning.

Daniel: Makes sense. In terms of the projects, the creative projects that came out as well as the processes you all were engaged in, do you feel like something really worked, something really one of the artistic projects or creative partnership projects, did it really work? Were there parts of the process or the project that didn't land within the Library Company?

Tania: Let's see. I would say that despite the struggle of the staff to keep up with just capacity wise, hours, numbers, timeline, that the artistic projects themselves were rather successful, the work that came out of it was really great work. Some of the connections that the artists were able to make with their audiences, they were really grounded connections.

I remember going to Tafari Robertson's opening, and he had invited his creative colleagues and friends to come in and speak and to offer their own work in the context of the Library Company. And talking to a couple of them in the reception who had never been in the building, didn't know that they were allowed to be in the building because of how it presents on the street, and also loved knowing the extent of the collection. A couple of them had gone to University of the Arts. They were young artists of color that they would've loved to come in and research some of these artists or some of these just sort of figures in African American culture and history had they realized that it was accessible to them. And so we talked about that a little bit. I think that was successful. [But] how to build on that?

I think that's one of the flaws in the project is that there is not a place to build on those small inroads that were made. And that was a struggle through the project in connecting to external audiences, in finding a process that connected to the external audiences. And I think for me, one of the questions I kept asking was sort of how you create a sense of value that, I'll come back to that word extractive, although it's overused right now, but who represents the project out in the world? How do you issue the invitation to participate? How you follow up on that invitation, how you sort of move beyond the thing that you're asking people to do and have them feel a valued part of that process in a way that allows them to continue our relationship with the organization?

I would say with Mark's project, there was a great response; I haven't followed up as much in terms of what came from those responses, but there are people who—looking at the Jennings painting, looking at the arc of what Mark did sort of in bridging the conversation between those two things—were just incredibly inspired, incredibly affected, deeply affected by what he produced.

I wasn't able to attend the We Are the Seeds performance, but I talked to the artists beforehand and the collaboration seemed really intriguing. We had one conversation about representation that I remember really clearly in trying to decide what images represented the project and talking about making decisions about those images, that the fact that the images existed didn't necessarily mean that they needed to be the thing that represented the project. So finding imagery that was more aspirational rather than the imagery that already existed.

And so I think there was a lot of value in the work that was done, and again, in sort of looking at the conversation we're having now, the question is how that translates—to a staff that is exhausted by this process, and to a wider audience where this information could be useful at the beginning rather than trying to wade through it after they've taken it on.

Bill: Yeah, I think I would just basically say the same thing with different words. I think the projects were really good; they were really effective. And the sad thing is that the effectiveness of those projects and the emotional gain for the institution, emotional and mental and intellectual gain for the institution was lost in all of the mess around making the project happen right from the very beginning. And I was just thinking about what would it have been like if all of those projects had been able to happen within an institution that wasn't facing a leadership, and a financial crisis, and what an impact it could have had. Because I think in people's minds, I mean, I certainly think in Sarah's mind and many others like it and being forced on them. And the staff has shrunk, and Mike left and Emily left, all of that is completely wrapped up with what they learned and whether the project was a good idea in the first place.

Daniel: But you all both interact with a lot of different organizations, and I think both have a literacy in how organizations work and that even though there's particularities here that there's a lot of staff turnover in organizations of this kind generally, there's a lot of budget issues and leadership transitions, and all these things happen all the time. And so what are the lessons learned in terms of how do you do ambitious projects, still do your daily work and also grow and evolve in ways that are not only urgently needed, but also can satisfy the demands both internally and externally of what it means to be relevant?

Tania: I would say there needs to be a lot more attention to the preparation for the project. I think for most people, the idea that we're going to have an artist or whatever the proposal is, or we're going to engage with community and the imagination that it's going to take some phone calls and some emails to get everything moving smoothly. I think people are not asking enough thoughtful questions about exactly what the process is going to entail. And one of the things that I think would be really helpful is building handbooks or whatever, but maybe I think a set of guidelines, if you intend to reach out to community partners.

And we're working on it with ArtPhilly. If these are our values and these are the things we want to accomplish, what are the working practices that allow them to come to the forefront? What are the working practices that allow things to move in the direction that we want without unduly taxing our staff? What are the understandings we have about what this will take and how we want to go about doing it? And it's a longer process than I think people would prefer it to be, but if it's going to have any value at all, we have to pay attention to the time and the relationships that matter.

Daniel: Thanks. That's great. You want to close out with anything, Bill?

Bill: This project, it was a perfect storm in a lot of ways, of wrenches thrown at it. But I was just thinking at the Rosenbach, we didn't have leadership and financial crisis and there was still a lot of resistance to these kinds of projects. But I think that goes back to what Tania said in terms of preparation. I didn't know enough when I was doing those projects to create a long enough warm-up or runway with the staff, with my colleagues, so that there could have been more buy-in and less resistance. I just went ahead and did them and it was fine, except that it created staff tension, which just meant everything took more energy than it needed to. But also, and then when I left, they stopped doing it. They were like, "good riddance to you and your stupid ideas" rather than actually having a real impact, long-term impact on the organization.

Daniel: Certainly I think that there's a scenario where that happens in this case, but I also would be interested to think about maybe, and maybe this is what this process of making a publication can do, maybe there sort of is a Cliff's Notes version of things that gets circulated to staff. They don't want to read a book about it, but maybe there is sort of a synthesis of some lessons learned that can be shared.

Bill: Or recommendations? Even like a list of recommendations. If you want to try a project like this, do these things, don't do these things.

Tania: I was looking, looking back at all my notes as we're speaking, and I think [another suggestion would be to get] a sense of the value of the staff input and reservations. Looking at from my first conversation, the staff, they were asking all the right questions, but maybe there was not time or the kind of attention that allowed them to come through. I was looking at the staff capacity. They were asking about the labor of the accessibility and community and diversity, who's accountable for the missteps, whether there were any issues of physical safety in terms of access to the building. And they talked a lot about morale. It was a difficult time at the institution. So sort of how to work through that in order to bring this process on.

And then they had questions about the institution, what the intended impact was, whether this was performative, whether they were going to be resources committed in the long term, how it could be informed by their own experiences to increasing the relevance of the collection and future capacity; what the right conversations are; how to coordinate with partners. There were a lot of questions that came up and that [revealed] the anxiety of taking the project on. And I think creating a space for all of those questions to come up to, to value all of the asking and attempting to answer all of the questions, no matter how simplistic they might seem. Bill's heard me say this before. We're always limited by our experiences. And I think bringing that into the conversation and understanding that people are allowed to come from whatever backgrounds they have with or without any degree of experience, and we can't punish them for not having the experience we would prefer. We can just try to ask good questions.

Bill: I think that I still believe that the organization will be different from now on. I still think that organizations are elastic. I think there was expansion.

Excerpted Hotline Transcripts From Rowhome Productions

The Library Company engaged the Philadelphia-based audio firm Rowhome Productions to implement an audience engagement component for the final "Beyond Glass Cases" project exhibition, "Reflections." Team members created questions that did not require any previous involvement with "Beyond Glass Cases" and a dedicated telephone hotline was established. During the exhibition's run from March 18-July 3, 2025 responses were shared at a listening station in the Library Company's gallery. All of the audio files are now available on the "Beyond Glass Cases" website https://librarycompany.org/bgc-reflections/.

QUESTION 1: What is gained and what is challenging about the Library Company or other libraries and museums undertaking projects that openly critique American history or even the institutions themselves?

> Response 01: The gains and challenges of critical projects at institutions like the Library Company are many times two sides of the same coin. They cause discomfort that can be generative in facilitating folks to care about the history of this country, albeit positively or negatively. The past, present, and future are intertwined, and if one participant in such a project is affected to delve beyond and/or question what they bear witness to, that is a win.
>
> Response 02: Maybe what's lost is a little bit of innocence. I think that a lot of us grew up with a thought of who we were as a country, and so there is [an innocence] that comes with that, but I don't think that [losing it] has to be a bad thing. So just perspective. Voices are invited into the room, which is really important too. So much of what was written down is just white and most often male. So also having other voices in the room is a very edifying thing.
>
> Response 04: I'm so excited that the Library Company's doing this right now because I feel like there are a lot of institutions in Philadelphia that are, really full of colonial-era history and history that is kind of further back and is maybe, I don't wanna say mainstream, but almost more mainstream. And I loved when I saw the Library Company was doing this and kind of delving into other kinds of history and like historical critiques, what is gained and lost.

Response 07: I think everything is gained and everything is challenging. I think that the gain is part of the educational mission that I think should be part of all these kinds of institutions. You really gain something by challenging people and, and you teach people by, you know, presenting something that they, in a way they hadn't thought about before. But in the same way, that can also be challenging because people might come to an exhibit expecting to see a history they're familiar with, and when they're presented with something that looks different from that, they have a reaction. And that's the challenging part.

Response 08: The most rewarding portion of what the Library Company and museums are doing is allowing people to think critically about some of the work that's already seen and showcased in some of the collections. The "Beyond Glass Cases" and day one—when we first walked into the Library Company, it was a very striking painting that has something where it's, dealing with slavery. I'm an African American woman, so that's very challenging to see and what the interpretation of that painting was...

I think when projects have an open critique about American history, we start to think about, again, as a millennial, as Gen Z, about what our history is and how we can do better at it. But that's the point of having collections, the point of having libraries, the point of having institutions. So if they're gone, we don't know what it is that we need to gain or something that we need to feel challenged about so we can do better over time.

Response 09: Well, people's feelings can get hurt. That's not always fun. And plus you have to admit that history is not perfect and that America might be fallible, that we've made some mistakes.

Response 10: What is gained when institutions take on projects that critique themselves or American history is a more complete understanding of the history. And that is what makes history interesting—its complexities both good and bad. I think the challenge when institutions take on projects like this is even in the best of times, they risk potentially offending supporters who might withhold financial support of them. In the current climate, I think the challenge is that a lot of institutions are afraid to give a critical look at American history for fear of drawing attention to themselves. Clearly what is wanted now is positive stories about American history told from a single perspective, and that perspective is a white male voice.

Response 11: Taking responsibility for past histories and not brushing that past history under the carpet. Being transparent and open. It's really important. And I think other institutions see that; the public sees that. And I think it's only a positive thing, a good thing, and speaking to truth is also a good thing. But it can be challenging as it can be uncomfortable bringing these uncomfortable past histories to the surface, which for years have been hidden from sight.

Response 12: What's gained is authentic and honest history. The way Americans have been taught history is very immature and too simplistic. It's often framed as good guys versus bad guys when humanity and history are just more complex and complicated than that. The challenge is people accepting and learning about some of the darker sides of our past, which people may not like.

They may need to confront previously held beliefs. There are no perfect people. So sometimes if they put people on a pedestal or they're heroes, especially like the founders like George Washington or Thomas Jefferson, they may get upset to learn about some of the more complicated and dark sides of those people's pasts.

Response 13: I think it's important for museums and libraries to try to interpret the materials they have in their collections. A lot of people want that sort of guidance when they visit, and a lot of people don't have the framework or the everyday access to such materials in order to make their own informed decisions about such things. And they're looking for that kind of guidance, I believe, from museums and libraries.

Response 14: What is gained is an enhanced knowledge of our history and also the inclusion of different voices into the stories of our history. What is gained is a change in perspective. What is gained is a deeper understanding of who we are, how we got there, how we might solve our problems, and how we might consider the future. Also what is gained is empathy, understanding for people different from ourselves, and also just an understanding of the other things that we may have missed and a feeling of vulnerability and hopefully openness to rethinking the things we just assume are true and building our muscles of inquiry and curiosity.

What is the risk? Alienating donors, making people feel uncomfortable. I think those are good, but that is the risk. Confusing people, making people feel unsettled with what they thought was true. That's the risk. Making people see that perhaps who they felt were their heroes are not so perfect after all.

Response 15: I think that a good museum presents the information in a way that consistently and fully describes the facts, allowing the audience to make their own conclusions about whether the information tells a story about a positive or negative impact on history. I think that it's not a museum's job to make a judgment, but rather to present the facts in such a way where the audience themselves can make their decisions.

QUESTION 2: Should libraries and museums strive to strike a balance in displaying collections that tell both positive and critical stories about history? Should controversial or offensive items ever be placed on public display, or should they be brought out only by specific request?

Response 01: Balance seems ideal but is not always appropriate depending on the moment or the subject. History is not objective and is affected by who is providing a narrative and who is engaging with it. I think there is import to displaying controversial items so that what they represent about our history is not forgotten. How they are displayed and the context in which they are provided will not be the same for these materials, and accountability is key.

Response 04: Yes. I think it depends, it's a difficult question because who is defining the balance and who is defining what's positive and what's negative. And I'm tempted to say, you know, a museum or a library should tell a full, a comprehensive story, which would include things that upset people and things that excite people and make them happy. So I'm reluctant to like engage in a conversation about it, where things are so bifurcated into things that are good and things that are bad. Positive histories, negative histories. I think the Library Company and other museums should really try to tell the complete story to the extent that they're able, regardless of the valence of opinion.

Response 05: Well, I'm a believer in true transparency. I don't think we should hide our past or, you know, I think it creates mistrust. We gotta take the good but the bad. You know, there's a lot of, particularly American, history that I don't think we've really reconciled as a country or even a civilization.

Response 06: Based on what I saw in the presentations that I saw, especially the "Crania Americana" piece, I think one way to answer that question is to say that archives and libraries and spaces like the Library Company do need help in terms of making those decisions. And unless you're gonna pay someone full time to be curator, which is a, you know, a significant investment, and maybe it's not even best to have just one person doing it.

Response 07: I don't know if balance is the right word because I don't necessarily think you need a completely equal measure of positive and critical stories about history. But look for the intersections. And I think controversial or offensive items—it really depends on the context that they're placed in and the sort of care and perspective of the exhibit. The exhibit text, how you're setting it up for the visitors so that visitors who might be really emotionally affected by something aren't taken completely by surprise.

Response 08: Listen, I believe in the First Amendment, which is the right to have freedom of speech and art, as in any other collection where you are voicing an opinion. Yes, it does have an opportunity to strike a balance in collection that will not only challenge us, but also show the positivity of such works.

Our public discourse when it comes to learning new cultures and histories—again, a lot of these public schools are just not getting that education in that. So when we have institutions and free institutions where we can literally walk in, read, and digest information on our own, we then give the opportunity to the next generation to then spark questions, ask for reasoning, and also just get excited about the works.

Response 09: I do think that in the right context, you can display controversial or offensive items as long as they're explained in the right way. Libraries are not museums, so it's really hard to put those kinds of things into context. I think it's easier if you are a museum because that is part of your job.

Response 13: I think it's worthwhile for libraries to try to strike an objective position when telling stories and interpreting histories. And this sort of goes back to the first question, but I think it's useful at the very least in terms of trying to meet people halfway and trying to present a history. If it's all one point of view to the detriment of another point of view, people who harbor that second point of view will not be receptive to the stories or the histories being told. And so I think if there is at least an attempt to show both sides of the story or to be even-handed in how the history is presented, you have a chance, at least in maybe retaining different audiences from different spectrums of any particular position. I am not so sure.

I don't think that controversial items should be placed in public. I think it's challenging because, you know many people, again, when they're coming to see an exhibit, they want to know history and so on, but you don't want to surprise or offend audience goers coming into the library with something that they're not expecting to see or, or with a history that they're not prepared to perhaps live so personally. And so I think there ought to be ways of presenting histories without necessarily showing materials that are going to be so sensitive. At the very least, if they're going to be shown, there should be an awful lot of disclaimers or preparation given in advance to allow people to understand that these materials are there for educational purposes and not for other lurid purposes. And I think that it's better, or it's safer, at least for the libraries and museums if the items are brought out specifically by request only.

Response 14: This is a really good question. I think it can be on display, but they need context and also they need warnings. Can they ever work and be on display? I feel like they can, because if we don't display them, do people start to think that bad things haven't happened and they worry that that's another type of erasure that can lead to negating people's experiences and also repeating bad things. But I can understand how displaying things like that could be painful and traumatizing to people. So it needs sensitivity. I do think the explanations that go with it have to be large and, and hard to avoid. Because I've seen sometimes it's too small in other museum exhibitions.

Response 15: I think that only a museum can answer that question for themselves. And to do so, a museum needs to have a clear understanding of who they are, what their mission is, and who their target audience is. Now, these are all marketing concepts, but having a clear understanding of these concepts will allow a museum to tell a story in such a way that doesn't offend their target audiences even if the story itself has negative information in it. An example of that is the United States Holocaust Museum—the story is told very factually and presented to the audiences for their own judgment. And when there are certain aspects that some people, maybe younger audiences, might consider to be offensive, right? Maybe stories of death, those exhibits are covered, so a parent might choose to lift a child up if they wanted them to see it, but at the same time it would be the parent's decision versus a younger visitor's. So the information should be there. All facts should be included, but it has to be connected to the museum's mission and understanding of who they are, what story they're telling, who the target audience is, what lessons the target audience needs to take out of the exhibit. So it shouldn't just be you know, a judgment that the museum makes or we are going to tell this or include that or not include that. It has to be very clearly defined and a lot of leg work has to be put on it before the exhibit is placed for the viewership.

QUESTION 3: Do you think that the Library Company or other libraries and museums should engage in conversations about diversity, equity, and inclusion? Has your opinion on this changed in the last few years?

Response 01: Yes and yes. The current anti-DEI climate weighs heavy—so many institutions are feeling forced to capitulate through fear of lost funding and legal retribution. Fighting the good fight out in the open, or through spin, is necessary and perpetual.

Response 02: I think it's extremely important. I mean, I could tell you just based on my age, the history that I was taught was very much from a white perspective, and there's so much that I've learned since my formal schooling, about stories that were happening, perspectives that were different perspectives from those same time periods that I thought I knew.

And I do, I think it's very important to have those different voices. And gosh, DEI has become obviously such a…. There's been so much controversy built around it, people don't even understand it, I think. And so just also making sure that people understand that it's not just about Black and white. Not just about male and female. Like there's just a whole larger perspective from lots of different human beings who are involved in building this country and creating the history and all these events that we think we know, that we don't know the whole story of.

Response 03: Yes, because there are many stories that were never told because of institutional discrimination against people based on race or sex and sexual orientation. And so it's about time and yes, those stories should be told.

Response 04: I think they absolutely should engage in those conversations, which is why I have appreciated, I think I've seen like a real effort from the Library Company in the last few years to engage more with younger scholars, scholars of color, people who are doing research into topics that might not have ordinarily or in the past been in the library.

I think it's important because again, if you're gonna tell the entire story of a place or a time, it should include perspectives that are from a variety of kind of backgrounds. I don't know that it's totally changed over the last few years, but I think it's become something that most people are thinking about more, I would say in the last six months as we're confronted with an administration federally who is trying to limit DEI. It has probably steeled my own reserve, like my own reserves of interest in it. Like we should be doing more of this work because if it weren't so important, then this regime would not be trying to silence it.

Response 05: I'd like to see us do away with the term diversity, equity, inclusion, just do it. You know, we label stuff and when you label things some may not really fully comprehend what that label means. So I think there's a way to include a DEI filter without coming out and just saying it.

And, you know, even big businesses are struggling with this now, right? And it's almost become a dirty word, dirty words, and I just don't think that's fair. And I think one way to overcome that is to eliminate the terminology and just do what the organization or organizations feel is the right thing to do.

Response 06: Those terms have emerged recently. They will morph and they will change. So I think the better question is to say, for me, with these institutions is that, missions need to be alive. They need to be engaged from time to time. Change is all there is. And so I would say that political change is its own world. I think these institutions have a responsibility to think about what change means to them, their own changing mission, and to feel like it needs to be a dynamic thing. This is not a really good answer to your question, but I guess my point is to say that institutions like this need to think about politics, but not too hard.

Response 07: This is the question right now, which is so scary, but I think absolutely they should engage in those conversations. I think that history, we only know the history that we know because it's been framed around white men so largely, and that's also why the staff of museums look the way they look. And so I think, you know, those people aren't the focus of history because they're the only people who have ever existed. They're the focus of history for reasons. And I think for the same reasons, it's important to highlight other aspects of history, other historical actors. And I don't think my opinion on that has changed in the past few years, except maybe to grow stronger. But I've really always felt that way.

Response 08: I think the Library Company, and of course the other public free libraries and museums that we have in Philadelphia, should always continue the conversation about diversity, equity, inclusion, because that is just how the culture is always made, the culture and the way societal norms and history is made upon past works of influential individuals [and] from past works of artists.

I think, you know, when we learned about who Harriet Tubman was, who Martin Luther King was, we didn't have much to go on. They weren't elected officials, they were advocates. They were those who were in a struggle during a certain time. But we had pictures, we had artworks, we had testimonials. We had, you know, the path that Harriet Tubman took in order to get from the south to the north. We had the route that she took under the railroad in order to get back and then gain more so.

We can't really erase the conversation of diversity, equity, and inclusion because that is just how our country was built. It was built on plantations, on immigration. But more so on the soul of individuals who worked hard to make America what it is today, which is absolutely great.

Response 09: Yes, they absolutely should. And in the last few years, my opinion that they should has only grown.

Response 10: I think it is important for libraries and museums to talk about diversity, equity, and inclusion. And I think it's even more important now in the current political climate that is trying to eliminate diversity, equity, and inclusion with those words stripped out of government websites and publications.

And it leaves libraries and museums that think that this is important work, still trying to do it, but to fly a little bit under the radar while doing it for fear of drawing attention to themselves and being very unsure of what the consequences would be of that attention. So, I think it's even more important now than it has been in the past.

Response 11: Absolutely. It is vital now more than ever. Many institutions are bowing to governmental demands. I can completely understand why, but I think it's important not to be silent and to speak out about diversity, equity, and inclusion and how important it is right now.

Response 12: Institutions need to have values and principles that they uphold. In the last few years, I've been disappointed and upset by how many institutions were inauthentic in their words and deeds and actually caused more harm. Having more diversity on staff, and especially in positions of power and leadership, is more important and meaningful than performative actions and empty conversations.

Response 13: This is a very sensitive topic politically these days, which it shouldn't be. However, I think that my opinion has not changed over the past few years, and I did think and still think that it is worthwhile to engage in these conversations. There are valid points of view that are beyond the white male perspective. And they need to be heard. They need to be understood, and people need to empathize with other perspectives that they may not live in their daily lives. And it is, I think, a responsibility of libraries and museums to discuss such things, to talk about such things openly, and to provide a safe space where such things can be discussed, and can be presented in a way that hopefully will reach different audiences, or all audiences, I should say and perhaps other, and engage new audiences and groups of people to come into the library and to recognize that their story is being told as part of the larger American history.

Response 14: Yes, they absolutely should. And my opinion has changed because I believe it's more important than ever. I think these conversations are vital to our progress, to understanding each other, to making us a better and stronger country, and even just for our own humanity. I think these conversations are so important, and I think museums and places like the Library Company can play a really critical role at keeping these conversations going. And also bringing in not just exhibitions, but speakers and programs like the one I'm participating in right now [with this hotline]. Just getting people to stop and think. But I think diversity, equity, inclusion, these are my values, and I hope that institutions value them as well.

Response 15: I think that this is somewhat of a tricky question. I think that in the modern world, we see diversity and inclusion as being applicable to some groups, to some very specific groups. But at the same time in the world today, we have a myriad of groups, and so when you only include one or two groups in conversations about diversity and inclusion, that means that you might be excluding some other groups. And it goes back to your target audience. Who is your target audience? What story are you trying to tell? If your target audience falls within specific groups, and you don't include them in, then it might have a negative impact, right, on the museum's ability to attract your target audience to the exhibit.

QUESTION 4: Should building community be an important aspect of the Library Company's mission? For example, should we continue to collaborate with partners such as artists, musicians, and community activists? What are the advantages and disadvantages of creating these partnerships?

Response 01: Building community is important, although it may be cliché, it does really provide a fuller picture and accessibility to a wider group of individuals from the different perspectives. Disadvantages of such partnerships are that they are often short term and can feel performative and disingenuous with no long-lasting changes to the library's practical means to support its mission.

Response 02: So I will say I have enjoyed seeing responses from artists to items in the collection. And again, it's because what I've seen has not just been the perspective of someone whose voice ethnically may not have been included originally, but also the artist's perspective and their interpretation of things. I think the responses actually that I've seen here provide a different entry point for a lot of people. It's not always strictly academic, which I think is another thing that libraries have done really well—is it's not just about, you know, books that you can pull off from a shelf and experience by yourself, but there's this conversation that gets created by an artist's response to something or their reaction to something which I think leads to valuable community conversations. It does build community. So yeah.

Response 03: 110% of museums and libraries should continue to bring in artists, musicians, community activists, because it's also going to bring a different community into these museums and libraries that traditionally brought in the same folks. And so if music or art brings some different voices and different opinions in, we should do it.

Response 04: I think they should mostly because I sometimes think the Library Company exists outside of what people tend to think of as libraries. I work at Community College of Philadelphia. I was telling a colleague of mine about going to this event tonight, and they were like, what is that place? And the way I described it, it didn't necessarily fit with the way you describe libraries, right? Like my library, I live in Mount Airy. The Lovett Library is like a community gathering space. There's programming, like there's stuff for kids, there's stuff for families. There's all kinds of events. And I think that the average Philadelphian doesn't necessarily look at the Library Company as having those same kind of community core values that your every day [library] like Free Library of Philadelphia would host.

So I think the more that the Library Company can engage in those kind of partnerships and collaborations, it will probably help attendance and engagement from the city.

Response 05: The answer to that question is absolutely yes. Think of like a local example; look what the Ensemble Arts has done, right? By bringing together the theater and music community on the Avenue of the Arts, I think that's a great example of how institutions can collaborate and create a community that kind of crosses you know, all genres of theater or presentation or performance. And I think libraries and art museums can, and many do, do the same.

Response 06: Well, my answer is yes. I don't think there's any doubt that engaging those people, but those things cost funds and capacity. And so, you know, without funding it becomes very difficult. But I don't think these institutions are embedded in community, whether or not we acknowledge it or not.

And the Library Company of Philadelphia is a Philadelphia institution. So I think part of the tension here, I don't wanna say tension, but part of the struggle here is that we have something for everyone to use, but coming in that front door, getting into the space, knowing that you can use it, knowing that it's okay for you to come in and ask odd questions and see what the answers are, that's a challenge. Because when you look at the front door, it doesn't scream to you—"This is for you" unless you know it's for you. So that's a challenge the Library Company will have to continue to address.

I'm really happy that when I've come to these events, that the rooms have been full. And that the faces seem to be more diverse than just a standard day at the Library Company when I was working here.

Response 07: I think absolutely community should be an important aspect. I mean, Philadelphia is in the name, Library Company of Philadelphia. And so it's important to reflect and engage the city that we're in. I mean, we steward this. I say "we", 'cause I used to be an intern here. I'm not anymore. I don't speak from the Library Company.

But the Library Company and any other institution that's based in a city or you know, within a community is based within that community. So part of that is reflecting and engaging with the people who live there. But you know, I think there are mostly advantages to that. I can really see the only disadvantages being that sometimes engaging with people like community activists or artists and musicians with a really specific point of view can create controversy. But controversy can also create conversations. And I feel like that's what these institutions are all about—creating conversations within those communities. So it's, to me, it's win-win.

Response 10: Creating partnerships is very important and should be a part of the Library Company's mission. Partnerships bring important new voices into institutions. However, creating these kinds of partnerships can't be just a one-and-done sort of experience. Partnerships have to be part of a long-term institutional plan with support at all levels of the institution or else you as an institution are just using people and communities in what is a very insincere way.

Response 12: Building community is a positive thing. There are multiple communities, so identifying which community you wanna have meaningful and long-term engagement with is essential. Exploiting communities, especially marginalized communities, is more damaging than beneficial and helpful.

Response 13: I think it is important for libraries to try and build a sense of community. Doing this, for instance, collaborating with other partners like artists and musicians and community activists is a great way of trying to.... Well, it does several things, I guess. It builds community with these other institutions and other communities in the area. It also potentially can help to increase people's awareness of the library itself, you know, beyond its traditional, normal readers and visitors. And I think that, in that respect, it has many advantages to potentially give to the library, in terms of increasing its visibility and making others aware that it is a force for change and that it is an institution that can play a role in communities rather than simply lurking in the background with, you know, three or five people visiting each month. So I think the advantages are, by trying to work with communities, again, the advantages that can only help the library to reach new people.

The disadvantage, however, is that it's very challenging for existing library staff who are often overworked and don't have enough time to take on such projects can be very challenging to coordinate and to work with people who are offsite and have their own different responsibilities. I think that is a serious disadvantage that needs to be worked around somehow, and that's really just a matter of logistics. I think rather than it's not an active obstructive way of causing problems. It's just simply a matter of, [there's] not enough time in the day for the people involved to do what they hope to accomplish.

Response 14: I think they should continue, and I think the advantages are you are bringing more voices into the conversation, and I think the arts are critical means of expression or understanding the human experience, and also understanding our history and being able to present these stories in often different way than things are recorded just in a written record. So I think these collaborations can really enrich what institutions like the Library Company can offer, and I appreciate the Library Company's investment in these types of collaborations.

The downside is that you'll alienate people who feel afraid to hear diverse voices, that you'll have to manage some donors who may feel like it's not their mission. And I think the other risks are you may make mistakes, you may offend people, even when you're trying your best to include people, because when you collaborate with partners, you can't always know what your partner is going to do, so that's always a risk.

Response 15: From the marketing standpoint, all partnerships and all com-munications must be strategic. This means that once you know what your mission is and what your product is, and who your target audiences are, you want to enter into partnerships with artists and community leaders who will help you to reach your target audiences so that the museum can benefit and tell the stories that it wants to tell in a productive way. So [the] museum has to do some legwork to understand what its identity looks like and then create those strategic partnerships that will advance and benefit the museum's long-term mission and goals.

QUESTION 5: If you participated in a "Beyond Glass Cases" program, such as a workshop, listening session, or public event, did you feel your experience was worthwhile or that your participation was respected and acknowledged? If not, what would have made the experience better for you?

> Response 02: I've walked past this place a million times, so having the opportunity to come in for the first time for this exhibit gave me a new perspective on what the Library Company was.
>
> Response 06: I went to the first event and the [event] at Asian Arts Initiative, and I didn't go to the last event. The night of the one event that I went to, I didn't like that, for whatever reason, those first two events, there wasn't senior leadership there. It was just the curatorial staff. And that would be my critique, because this program is really cutting edge and there's a lot of money, with the Pew stuff on the ground. So, that would be my one comment on that. Otherwise, I thought they went really well. They felt really good. And yeah, especially with the musical piece, I'm really glad I was there and I got to meet Julian and it was very, it was an emotional evening.
>
> Response 08: I will say I did participate in a listening session for "Beyond Glass Cases" program. It was certainly worthwhile. It was moderated by someone who actually knew the lay of the land of how Philadelphia works, but also knew what the artwork and the premise of some of the pieces that they were talking about in the collection. It was a well-rounded conversation with a group of individuals who had a stake somewhere. So you had somebody that worked in education, somebody worked in government, somebody worked in public service accounting, and we were all sitting at the table engaging on the same topic with different backgrounds and experiences.
>
> Response 13: Yes, I did participate and I did observe various [projects] during the time the "Beyond Glass Cases" exhibits were up. I also attended the "Crania Americana" video presentation. I have to say, I guess, I do think my experiences were worthwhile. I should say, that I am personally, and this is just my, perhaps my own failing, but I'm always a little resistant or my shields go up when art is involved because I'm not necessarily comfortable and don't feel that I always understand where art is coming from, but I think that that's the point of art, frankly. And so forcing myself to be made uncomfortable is probably a good thing. So I thought some of the events were more successful than others. I did really enjoy Mark Thomas Gibson's exhibit, and I did also enjoy and feel I learned a lot from the "Crania Americana" exhibits. I did really actually feel myself being brought into

the experience and trying to understand history from a perspective that's different from my own. And, again, that's something intellectually that I already agree with but the performance was helpful because it really did bring it, make it a little more alive and real and to recognize the emotion behind the intellectual understanding.

CREDITS AND ACKNOWLEDGEMENTS

'Beyond Glass Cases: The Library Company of Philadelphia's "Collections Lab"' has been supported by The Pew Center for Arts & Heritage. The views expressed are those of the author(s) and do not necessarily reflect the views of The Pew Center for Arts & Heritage, The Pew Charitable Trusts, or the Barnes Foundation.

"Beyond Glass Cases" was served by an external advisory committee composed of a diverse group of cultural heritage thought leaders. These advisors were: Bill Adair, Dr. Anne Bowler, Catherine Cooney, Tania Isaac Hyman, Lois Stroehr, and Neferteri Strickland.

"Beyond Glass Cases" was supported by numerous current and past Library Company of Philadelphia staff members including: Linda Kimiko August, Dr. Michael Barsanti, Ruth Scott Blackson, Rachel D'Agostino, Sophia Dahab, Fran Dolan, Dana Dorman, Wynn Eakins, Esther Ellis, Connor Feeney, Dr. Carleton Gholz, Abigail Guidry, Emily Guthrie, Raechel Hammer, Grace Harrington, Sharon Hildebrand, Alison Kronstadt, Addie Peyronnin, Brandon Pinzini, Erika Piola, Jose Placeres, Dan Shiman, Dr. John C. Van Horne, and Sarah Weatherwax.

"Beyond Glass Cases" benefited from the support of numerous external partners including:

Tailihn Agoyo and We Are the Seeds, Alex Azar, Asian Arts Initiative, barb barnett graphic design llc, Ian Bosak, Common Ground Research Networks, Eric Marsh, Sr., Shannon Mattern, Pueblo, Alex Lewis and John Myers of Rowhome Productions, and TML Communications.

"Lineage" listening session participants included Philadelphia high school history teachers; high school students from the social justice media program POPPYN; community leaders attending the political education program Du Bois Movement School for Abolition & Reconstruction; and volunteers from the Paul Robeson House and Museum.

The Black Historians' Salon contributors included: Sweet Corey-Bey, Ajon Jones, and Blue Sankofa. The "Black Historians' Department" variety show participants included: Chris Arnold, Black Buttafly, Sherry Howard, Jade Walker, and Ayanna Woods.

Photography Credits: Images in this book were taken by
Jaci Downs
Sharon Hildebrand
Max Macdonald
Editorial Advisor: Sarah Weatherwax.
Cover design by barb barnett graphic design llc.

Acknowledgments

From Sarah Weatherwax: Thanks are extended to The Pew Center for Arts & Heritage for funding this project, and in particular to Alec Unkovic, Program Officer for Visual Art & Creative Practices, who served as the project liaison to the Library Company throughout the entire project.

From Daniel Tucker: Thanks to Bill, Sarah, and Tania for bringing me onto this fascinating project. Thanks to Phillip and Tracy at Common Ground Research Networks for your partnership in publishing. Thanks to Dan S. Wang for being an outside reader and friend. Thanks to Emily for your support and discussion. And thanks to Bay who napped while I developed this book and for being the best baby in the world.

CONTRIBUTORS

Bill Adair, Senior Advisor to "Beyond Glass Cases", is the Creative & Executive Director of ArtPhilly. He has over two decades of experience as a practicing museum curator and educator, most recently at the Rosenbach Museum & Library in Philadelphia, where he began an artist-in-residence program, commissioned several new media projects, and produced a range of educational and public programs. Bill has a BA in History from the University of Pennsylvania and an MA in Cultural Planning and Policy from the University of California, Los Angeles. He is coeditor of the book "Letting Go? Sharing Historical Authority in a User Generated World" (Left Coast Press, 2012).

Linda Kimiko August joined the Library Company of Philadelphia staff in 2004. She is a graduate of Widener University with a BA in History and an MA in Museum Communication from the University of the Arts. Ms. August is a Visual Materials Cataloger in the Graphic Arts Department and the Curator of the Art & Artifacts Collection, which contains over 300 cultural objects, including paintings, sculpture, decorative arts, and scientific instruments. She spearheaded a multiyear project to digitize and catalog the Art & Artifacts Collection and conserve a number of important pieces by successfully attaining grants from the National Endowment for the Arts (NEA) and the Pennsylvania Historical and Museum Commission (PHMC). She co-curated the exhibition "Together We Win: The Philadelphia Homefront During the First World War" and curated "Stylish Books: Designing Philadelphia Furniture." Her research interests include the history of the Library Company, the artifacts in the collection, and Asian American history.

Rachel D'Agostino joined the Library Company in 2000, where she serves as Curator of Printed Books, previously having worked as Reference Librarian and in the Cataloging and Administration departments. Rachel holds an MLS from Clarion University, as well as a Master of Theological Studies degree from Harvard Divinity School and a BA in Religion from Temple University. In 2013, she co-curated the Library Company's exhibition "Remnants of Everyday Life: Historical Ephemera in the Workplace, Street, and Home." She followed this in 2016 with "Common Touch: The Art of the Senses in the History of the Blind", in 2022 with "Hearing Voices: Memoirs from the Margins of Mental Health", and in 2025 with "Fair Winds and Following Seas: Peacetime Naval Operations to 1939." Rachel has taught numerous classes on book history and book arts, served as Senior Lecturer at the University of the Arts, and is a lab instructor in descriptive bibliography at Rare Book School at the University of Virginia.

Mark Thomas Gibson brings a multifaceted lens to American culture—as a Black man, professor, and history enthusiast—using drawing, painting, print, and sculpture to explore a satirical, dystopian vision of the United States where viewers become characters in the unfolding narrative. Born in Miami in 1980, he is an assistant professor in Art & Design at Mason Gross School of the Arts, Rutgers University. He is represented by M+B (Los Angeles) and Loyal (Stockholm). In 2021, Gibson was awarded a Fellowship from the Pew Center for Arts & Heritage, Philadelphia, PA, and a Hodder Fellowship from the Lewis Center for the Arts, Princeton University, Princeton, NJ. In 2022, Gibson was awarded a Guggenheim Fellowship from the Guggenheim Memorial Foundation, New York, NY, and was named a 2022 Grantee by The Louis Comfort Tiffany Foundation New York, NY. Notable curatorial projects include "Black Pulp!" (2016, with William Villalongo) and "Edge of Echoes" (2024, Jenkins Johnson Gallery). His artist books include "Some Monsters Loom Large" (2016) and "Early Retirement" (2017). His first monograph will be published in 2025 by JRP Editions in conjunction with his exhibition "Overture" at The Berman Museum.

Emily Guthrie is the Abby and George O'Neill Executive Director of the John D. Rockefeller Jr. Library at Colonial Williamsburg and the former Librarian of the Library Company of Philadelphia. Emily was previously at Winterthur, where she was the Library Director since 2017 and NEH Librarian for the Printed Book since 2009. Emily earned a BFA in historic preservation from the Savannah College of Art & Design in 1997. In 2001, she returned to school to earn an MSLS from the School of Information and Library Science at the University of North Carolina at Chapel Hill.

Sharon Hildebrand joined the Library Company staff as the Lea Family Head of Conservation in September 2022. For fourteen years prior, she has served as Head Preparator for Works on Paper at the Philadelphia Museum of Art. Her previous positions include various book and paper conservation and preservation roles at the American Philosophical Society, the Historical Society of Pennsylvania, as well as an earlier stint at the Library Company. She studied bookbinding and printmaking at the Oregon College of Art and Craft. Her research interests include sewn-board bindings, historical endbands, and publisher cloth bindings. Sharon teaches bookbinding and book arts classes and workshops and is a member of the Guild of Book Workers and the Philadelphia Center for the Book.

Tania Isaac Hyman is a former Pew Fellow and McDowell Fellow a choreographer, dancer, writer who has led international performances while creating models for thoughtful, audience-centered engagement. Her published writing explores the spectrum of contemporary dance ranging from essays and commentary to comparative esthetics in performance. Tania is a former Maggie Allesee National Center for Choreography Fellow, Pew Fellow, MacDowell Fellow, and Urban Leaders Fellow. She holds a Bachelor of Science in Dance from the University of Wisconsin-Madison, a Master in Fine Arts in Dance from Temple University, and a Master in Public Administration from the University of Pennsylvania's Fels Institute for Government. She is currently the Curatorial Director of ArtPhilly.

Zachariah Julian serves as the Digital Media and Artistic Producer for We Are the Seeds, a Philadelphia-based organization producing cultural events, programs, and workshops that celebrate and support Indigenous arts and artists throughout North America. He curates programs that are diverse, balanced, interesting, and entertaining. Zachariah composes music for From Here, With a View and other Seeds programs. Additionally, Zachariah edits daily content to upload to We Are the Seeds social media and archives and is a podcast producer and host. A musician and performer, he is knowledgeable in production and stage management. He has lived on the Apache Nation for nineteen years and has been playing piano for over twenty years. Zachariah started composing when he was sixteen years old and attended University of New Mexico majoring in Music Theory and Composition. He has just released a record titled "Oblique".

Shannon Mattern is the Director of Creative Research at the Metropolitan New York Library Council, a state-founded, member-supported, nonprofit network connecting hundreds of libraries and archives. In Spring 2025, she was the Kluge Chair in Modern Culture at the Library of Congress, a position nominated by the Librarian of Congress herself. Prior to her work with METRO, she held full professorships in media studies, anthropology, and art history at The New School and the University of Pennsylvania. Mattern's writing and teaching focus on archives, libraries, and other media spaces; media infrastructures; sites where data intersect with art and design; and media that shape our sensory experiences. She is the author of four books: "The New Downtown Library: Designing with Communities"; "Deep Mapping the Media City"; and "Code and Clay", "Dirt and Data: 5,000 Years of Urban Media" (winner of the Anne Friedberg Innovative Scholarship Award from the Society for Cinema and Media Studies and the Dorothy Lee Award for Outstanding Scholarship in the Ecology of Culture from the Media Ecology Association), all published by the University of Minnesota Press; and "A City Is Not a Computer", published by Princeton University Press in 2021. https://wordsinspace.net/.

Paul Wolff Mitchell is an anthropologist and historian working on the histories and afterlives of scientific racism in museums, the anthropological collection of human remains, and theories of racial difference and human origins in the eighteenth and nineteenth centuries. He is a postdoctoral scholar at the University of Amsterdam with a project titled "Pressing Matter: Ownership, Value, and the Question of Colonial Heritage in Museums," funded by the Dutch Research Council (NWO). Paul has held fellowships from the Consortium for the History of Science, Technology, and Medicine; the McNeil Center for Early American Studies; the Library Company of Philadelphia; the Fulbright U.S. Program; the German Academic Exchange Service; and the Wenner-Gren Foundation. He has also been a research fellow with the Penn and Slavery Project and the Penn Program on Race, Science and Society. His research has been covered in "Discover, Forbes, The Guardian", and the "New York Times".

Erika Piola is the Curator of Graphic Arts and Director of the Visual Culture Program at the Library Company of Philadelphia. She has worked in the Graphic Arts Department at the Library Company since 1997. She received her BA from Haverford College and her MA in History from the University of Pennsylvania. She is Director of the Visual Culture Program and has served as a project director and curator for a number of Library Company initiatives, including "Imperfect History", "Common Touch", "Philadelphia on Stone", eighteenth-and-nineteenth-century ephemera, and African Americana graphics. She is editor and contributor to "Philadelphia on Stone: Commercial Lithography in Philadelphia, 1828–1878" (Penn State University Press, 2012). Ms. Piola has also presented and published work on American visual culture, nineteenth-century ephemera, the antebellum Philadelphia print market, and the Library's African American history and photography collections. Her research interests include Philadelphia lithography, the frame maker and print dealer James S. Earle, print seller Sarah Hart, and stereographs portraying the New Woman.

Tafari Robertson is a multidisciplinary artist based in Philadelphia, PA. He began his artist journey through painting, illustration, and he now works across mediums to explore the experiences layered within Black cultural spaces. He questions what are the artistic effects of space, the elements that create those experiences, and what ripples out when these spaces are created, sustained, or destroyed. His Book Space Archive is a series of audio collages developed through an investigative oral history practice conducted with historically Black bookstores across the United States. Through interviews with owners and patrons, he pieces together themes and histories to create a new conversation for audiences to engage with, highlighting the energies preserved in these spaces that have upheld Black culture and are too often lost without notice. Currently developing his speculative practice, his Future Forms explore the effects of administrative design toward creating perceptions of permanence and authority as pillars for institutional buy-in. He uses this work to build on the imaginative possibilities of creating new worlds for those ignored or diminished in our current frameworks.

Daniel Tucker works extensively in the museum and public art fields and helps artists, activists, and organizations to create impactful work. He has done this through creating innovative publications, academic programs, dynamic gatherings, and critical exhibitions. His last coauthored book "Lastgaspism: Art and Survival in the Age of Pandemic" (Soberscove, 2022) was picked as a "Best Art Book of 2022" by Hyperallergic. He has led graduate programs in museum studies and socially engaged art for the last decade and is the Research Network Chair of the international Arts in Society Research Network. He recently organized the Curating Engagement Retreat with support of Wagner Foundation and Public Trust. Since 2023, he has organized the ongoing Eco-Social Salon, Site-Seeing, and Screening Series in Philadelphia.

John C. Van Horne was Director of the Library Company from 1985 to 2014 and returned as Director in 2024. He holds a bachelor's degree in history from Princeton University and a master's degree and doctorate in history from the University of Virginia. He was elected to the American Philosophical Society in 2005. Dr. Van Horne's publications include a dozen articles, many volumes of "The Papers of Benjamin Henry Latrobe (Yale)" and other edited works such as "Religious Philan-thropy and Colonial Slavery: The American Correspondence of the Associates of Dr. Bray, 1717–1777 (1985)"; "The Abolitionist Sisterhood: Women's Political Culture in Antebellum America (with Jean Fagan Yellin, 1994)"; "Traveling the Pennsylvania Railroad: The Photographs of William H. Rau (2002)"; and "America's Curious Botanist: A Tercentennial Reappraisal of John Bartram (1699–1777) (with Nancy Hoffmann, 2004)".

Sarah Weatherwax is Senior Curator of Graphic Arts at the Library Company of Philadelphia. Sarah has worked at the Library Company of Philadelphia since 1993. She received a BA in History from the College of Wooster (Ohio) and a

MA in History from the College of William and Mary. She has published articles in the "Daguerreian Annual, The Magazine Antiques, Pennsylvania History", and "Imprint: The Journal of the American Historical Print Collectors Society", and contributed a chapter about lithographer Peter S. Duval to "Philadelphia on Stone: Commercial Lithography in Philadelphia, 1828–1878". She has curated exhibitions on topics as diverse as Philadelphia daguerreotypes, the Philadelphia homefront during World War One, Federal artist William Birch, and most recently "Imperfect History". Other research interests include women in photography and Philadelphia's built environment. She currently serves on the board of the American Historical Print Collectors Society.

www.ingramcontent.com/pod-product-compliance
Lightning Source LLC
Chambersburg PA
CBHW041935260326
41914CB00010B/1312